£23-00

370.1523
Jon

Blueprint
for
Student
Success

076946977 1

Dedicated to the giving people all around—the teachers who raise the hair on my arms when I witness them work their magic with a child. And to the best teacher of all—Mom.

Blueprint for Student Success

A Guide to Research-Based Teaching Practices K-12

SUSAN J. JONES

CORWIN PRESS, INC.
A Sage Publications Company
Thousand Oaks, California

For information:

Corwin Press, Inc.
A Sage Publications Company
2455 Teller Road
Thousand Oaks, California 91320
www.corwinpress.com

Sage Publications Ltd.
6 Bonhill Street
London EC2A 4PU
United Kingdom

Sage Publications India Pvt. Ltd.
B-42 Panchsheel Enclave
Post Box 4109
New Delhi 110 017 India

Printed in the United States of America

Library of Congress Cataloging-in-Publication Data

Jones, Susan J.
Blueprint for student success: a guide to research-based teaching practices K-12 / Susan J. Jones.
    p. cm.
Includes bibliographical references and index.
ISBN 0-7619-4697-7 (cloth)
ISBN 0-7619-4698-5 (pbk.)
   1. Learning, Psychology of. 2. Teaching. 3. Academic achievement.
I. Title.
LB1060 .J67 2003
370.15′23—dc21

2002151360

This book is printed on acid-free paper.

03   04   05   06   07   7 6 5 4 3 2 1

Acquisitions Editor:	Faye Zucker
Editorial Assistant:	Julia Parnell
Production Editor:	Olivia Weber/Julia Parnell
Typesetter/Designer:	C&M Digitals (P) Ltd
Indexer:	Jean Casalegno
Cover Designer:	Tracy E. Miller
Production Artist:	Sandra Ng Sauvajot

Contents

Preface

The education profession speaks of lifelong learners, but perhaps I am a lifelong *teacher* as well. After two decades in the classroom and years beyond in professional development, I still hunger for ways to "do it better." My focus has sharpened, transitioning away from a desire to be the best teacher toward wanting to *teach the best*: to facilitate and maximize learning for every child.

This quest has led me to countless seminars and workshops and hundreds of publications. Taken together with personal experience, they serve as the foundation for better understanding of excellence in learning strategies: techniques and processes that are effective and practical. Yet observation of teachers in action reinforces one other belief: that even with the best textbooks, the finest equipment, and the most modern physical plant, the learning environment must, first and foremost, be equipped with the finest teachers, fully informed and trained in best practice. I hold an unwavering belief that the primary teaching tool is the teacher. He or she can make the difference between student learning and student failure; between mediocrity or excellence in student growth and achievement.

This book approaches best practice instructional delivery through practical strategies and techniques, organized by categories, that can be adopted and adapted by any teacher at any learning level. The categories are what have resonated with me the most, as I have scoured literally hundreds of research-based books and journals related to teaching, learning, and the human brain. It is a synthesis of that which appears to me as critical to sound instruction. The activities in this book, although not individually validated by research in the cognitive neurosciences, try to respect the general leanings of research. If teachers can acquire a better understanding of the essentials of good teaching, then the possibilities for solid learning may increase. In my extensive staff development experience, I find folks appreciate programs and theory, but ask, "What does it look like in a classroom? How would I use this idea?" Therefore practical applications are provided so educators can envision new techniques in their own classrooms. They can be borrowed and adapted to the unique characteristics of any classroom and any learner.

My bottom line? That student achievement is raised. The greatest compliment paid to me professionally is that I really do what I preach. I am hoping that my book does the same—that it does what *it* preaches and that is to make instruction powerful and learning easier for every single child.

This book serves to empower teachers.

ACKNOWLEDGMENTS

Corwin Press wishes to thank the following reviewers:

Nancy Melucci
Instructor, PACE Program
Los Angeles Harbor College
Wilmington, CA

Margo Marvin
Director of Curriculum and Technology
Windsor Locks Public Schools
Windsor Locks, CT

Elizabeth Lolli
Director of Curriculum
Mayfield City Schools
Stow, OH

Angie Roman
Director of Special Services
Windsor Locks Public Schools
Windsor Locks, CT

Bonnie Watson
Middle School Writing Specialist
Owensboro Middle School
Owensboro, KY

Robert Sylwester
Emeritus Professor of Education
University of Oregon
Eugene, OR

About the Author

 **Susan Jones** has helped over 25,000 educators translate the results of brain research into practical strategies for teaching and learning. Her no-nonsense approach to instruction and leadership separates critical new research from speculation and skillfully presents the elements that positively impact achievement. She serves on the Board of Directors of ASCD, is President of the Florida ASCD, and is a trainer for the Bureau of Education and Research. She has also served as Director of Program Development for Illinois Regional Offices of Education. She has more than two decades of K-12 classroom teaching experience and teaches graduate-level courses through three universities. Her Web site is www.susanjjones.com.

1

Laying Groundwork for Learning

Meaning and Memory

Every day, in every way, I'm getting better and better.

—Èmile Couè, 1857–1926

Improvement makes straight roads.

—William Blake, 1757–1827

Learning is the business of education. Inherent in it is acquisition of knowledge and skill through a systematic study or experience. Learning, therefore, necessitates growth. And growth is change. Since educators are responsible for planning and carrying forward this systematic process, they must orchestrate environments conducive to learning. Yet any environment demanding change is fraught with risk and uncertainty. Setting a stage conducive to change, therefore, is critical. Successful school environments provide rich experience, safety for risk taking, and a positive climate to promote excitement for learning.

CONSTRUCTING MEANING
AND CREATING MEMORY

When a human experiences something for the first time, it is a primary experience. In response, brain nerve cells that perceive and process the new information fire, forming a unique communication between these nerve cells, or neurons, in response to the stimulation. This simultaneous firing forms a circuit for communication to process information. The result is a new pattern and combination of communication: a memory network involving sensation, emotional arousal, attentional focus, and perhaps eventually, problem solving and movement. Such a memory network is like a recipe for the experience or process. Each time the brain remembers, the network is refired and the memory is recalled. Recombining the ingredients into the "whole" re-creates the original experience, whether a thought or process. The resulting memory network then serves as a template for similar, subsequent experiences and becomes a measuring stick for understanding.

Take the example of a 9-month-old child sitting on a blanket in the park when a puppy comes running by. That pup might rush toward the baby, click its claws on the sidewalk, and excitedly sniff the child. It will smell like wet fur as it licks the baby's face, and its shaggy coat will rasp the child's cheek. Perhaps it's the first time that baby has ever come in contact with a dog. She may not understand the word *dog*, but her senses have been filled and her brain planted with a memory made possible by the instantaneous communication between numerous neurons firing in conjunction. The entire sensory and emotional memory of this creature has been planted.

A week may then pass until her parents take her to the zoo and she sees her first giraffe. The child will make a mental connection between it and the dog—and recognize patterns. They both have four legs, a snout, and floppy ears, and if she is old enough to speak, she may call the giraffe "doggy." She has measured the new experience against a prior one, using the template of meaning to understand. New information is reconciled with the old to reform or strengthen her individual concept of reality.

The same process takes place in school settings, as evidenced in the much-told joke about kindergartner Madison. Her teacher spends a full day discussing and demonstrating the concept of sets. At the dinner table that evening, Dad asks what she learned in school. Madison proceeds to describe the concept of "sets" that was a learning concept from that day:

> "Mrs. Smith had all the kids with shorts on stand against the wall: That was a set of kids with shorts. The kids who carried their lunches were asked to stand against the wall, and they were a set of kids who brought their lunches.
>
> "Madison," Mom asked, "see that bowl of green beans on the table? Could they be a set?"

"Well, Mommy, if they could get up and go stand against the wall . . ."

It is important, therefore, to determine each child's perceptions of reality and preconceived notions about concepts before beginning any instruction and then to recheck throughout the learning activity as well. Better understanding of a child's foundational and unfolding knowledge or perceptions enables the teacher to fine-tune instruction by speeding up, slowing down, re-explaining, or finding alternate ways of clarifying concepts.

ORGANIZING EXPERIENCES FOR UNDERSTANDING

Much of what is taught in schools involves declarative memory. These are factual names and places, types of memories that identify categories. As such, they involve language and consciousness and can be abstract or concrete: anything from mathematics to initial stages in skill acquisition, like dribbling a basketball (Sylwester, 1995).

As children grow to school age, their pool of life experience and understanding of the world is significant, due in great part to the accumulation of declarative long-term memories. To make sense of new learning experiences, the child will need multiple comparisons and contrasts between incoming information and patterns of earlier experience, all filtered through the screen of his or her personal truths. Previous experiences and their interpretations become the yardstick for current understanding. Activities 1.1 and 1.2 demonstrate activities that tap into a child's experiences and perceptions. Because recall involves the refiring of memory networks, intertwining and overlapping new stimulation with existing neural memory networks reveal patterns and the interrelatedness of the world.

 Activity 1.1   Silent Pass

Purpose: To ascertain a child's understanding of concepts prior to new instruction.

Write several questions or terms that are central to upcoming instruction, each on a separate card. Distribute one card to each student. Ask students to look at their term and think about its meaning or significance and record their thoughts on the card. Limit time to roughly 1 minute before directing students to trade cards with classmates to get a new term. Children should read and reflect on the new term and all ideas recorded by others. Then instruct them to add their

(Continued)

Activity 1.1 (continued)

own thoughts. Repeat the exchange/recording step again. The last time students trade cards, do not have them add their thoughts; instead, they will choose the idea already recorded on the card they hold that they find most significant or enlightening.

Ideas are shared for each term or question, with the teacher recording them on chart paper. Post all ideas publicly for referencing as instruction unfolds to either validate preconceptions or find inaccuracies in them. Not only does this allow the teacher to establish prior knowledge and spot strengths or misunderstanding, it is a safe discussion process for sharing ideas. Students take pride in reporting something they deem worthwhile, and as instruction unfolds, they can self-assess their own growth.

 Activity 1.2   Bounce Back

Purpose: To build on prior knowledge and refine old templates of student understanding.

Before beginning a unit of study for heavy content projects, tap prior knowledge by asking students to form groups of three to answer questions based on existing perceptions or knowledge. For instance, if initiating a lesson on blank verse poetry, ask students for the characteristics one expects in poetry. It is likely that they will mention features such as rhyming and defined rhythm. When the class reconvenes, record group ideas. Sort responses into separate categories or concepts and draw connections to that which you are about to teach. When instruction is delivered, refer back to their ideas to verify or refute them, always bouncing off their original concepts. The teacher can guide students to distinguish blank verse from other types of poetry as the lesson unfolds.

When a child understands the word *television* ("a visual sent over a distance"), it is easier for him or her to comprehend the basic meaning of a new word, *telepathy*. The child can intertwine that knowledge with other memory circuits that share a characteristic, like those involving the meanings of *telescope, telegraph, telegenic,* and *telekinesis.* Connecting new information to old, the brain's understanding of its world expands.

From birth to death, the brain tries to understand its world by measuring the new against the old. If an experience reaffirms a prior perception of the world, established "truths" are reinforced. All dogs have fur, and they slobber, click claws, and lick faces. Yet although experiences may be similar, they are never *identical*. A dog might have a pug face, not a long snout; a dog might not race and jump but, instead, lie sleeping. In the face of such contradiction, the brain either creates new subcategories of information (there are subsets of dogs: those that have long noses and those that have pug faces) or it rejects the new information because it does not fit with one's truth. The latter might be characterized as close-mindedness, generalization, stereotyping, or denial, whereas the former is growth and learning. Learning, then, *is* change: change in understanding through additional information to limit, expand, alter, or rework memory truths to more accurately depict the world.

Similarly, the learning that goes on in our classrooms involves expansion of understanding. A child notes a defined sound for the letter *t*, as in "tip," "top," and "toe." Repeated exposure reinforces the understanding that the symbol always makes the same sound—until the child is exposed to *-th* or *-tion*. Eventually, exposure to a foreign language might reveal even more possible categories of sounds: exceptions and, subsequently, new categories and subcategories as the world comes into focus.

Growth *is* change. As educators, it is imperative that we help students gain new experiences to reinforce, expand, and build neural networks through discovery (as in Activity 1.3), application, manipulation (as in Activity 1.4), creativity, and higher-level thinking. *That* is learning!

✳ **Activity 1.3**   Word Pulls

Purpose: To help primary-level children detect patterns in letter sounds and sequences.

Post an interesting photo or a colorful poster and invite children to "pull" words from the picture by sharing what they see. The teacher records the words children speak, repeating each letter as it is written (foot, bear, apple, etc.). This taps into student listening and speaking vocabularies to generate a list of written words.

Next, guide students to discover similarities between words on the list: For example, if the words *foot, wood, grass, loot, watermelon, board, hair,* and *curls* are recorded, children might note that *foot* and *wood* have double Os that make the same sound. The teacher then provides each student with a short passage of text containing several *-oo-* words, such as *hood, mood, toot,* or *soot*. Students are given this assignment: Find any *double-O* words and bring them back the next day. Through group discussion and word exploration, children will discover that not all -oo- words make exactly the same sound. They will expand their understanding by discovering patterns plus create new categories and subcategories. Expand and grow! A deepening repertoire (adapted from Calhoun, 1999).

✳ **Activity 1.4**   Patterns and Categories
_____

Purpose: To help students see patterns and make connections to hone editing skills, which are necessary for categorizing and classifying ideas.

Demonstrate how to form categories of everyday objects by selecting items from the classroom, perhaps three items chosen from the teacher's desk. Ask students why those items might have been put together: Are they all tools? Are they all plastic? Do they all have the color red on them? Can each be held in one's hand?

Next, give each group of two to four students a bag of items and ask them to arrange them into three different groups. Ask students to report their solutions to the class, explaining which feature items share within each group. Repeat the process, asking them to find new ways to arrange items. Each time, have students name the criteria or features that make the grouping sensible (e.g., buttons can be grouped by color, size, number of thread holes, materials—the sky is the limit!). Students begin to see how classifications and categories change as criteria do.

GROWTH AND LEARNING

Learning, then, involves actual physical change in a brain's architecture. New connections between neurons form memory networks that eventually intertwine as new relationships are realized. Discovering the same word root in *pentagon* and *pentameter* links forever two distinctly different networks of thought. One involves shape and one involves an element of poetry, but they are related through the glue of meaning. Learning the fingering of a clarinet makes playing a saxophone much easier. Growth comes by figuring out one's world through detection of patterns to gain understanding. The brain benefits from the big picture that serves as a touchstone for understanding. Only then do people get their bearings and feel safe.

2

Fertile Fields
for Learning

Supple as Cotton, Rigid as Steel

FRAMEWORK FOR SECURITY
WHERE CHANGE IS THE GOAL

Templates change as understanding of the world increases, with new experiences processed and then assimilated into all that has occurred before. "New" implies change, and change *means* risk. So how do we provide the necessary security in a classroom, where change *is* the normal state? There are three important avenues to a safe learning environment: atmosphere, rituals, and procedure.

POSITIVE CLASSROOM ENVIRONMENT

Traditionalists may wrinkle their noses in disgust at the concern over creating a positive atmosphere. Learning is tough, they say. And they are right; it is hard work. More brain energy is required to learn new ideas and skills than to recall, apply, or review existing ones. So anything that facilitates or encourages a learner to spend that energy is important.

In considering the learning environment, careful attention should be paid to conditions beyond those of temperature, noise, and physical layout (although all are important). A most critical quality of any learning environment is the teacher's approach in delivering instruction and directing learning. Communication must be positive—not just with words chosen, but with gestures and expressions that demonstrate acceptance of individuality. Humans know how others feel, with or without the expression of words (Peoples, 1992). Fifty-five percent of the impact of social communication is visual (energy, movement), whereas 38% of the impact comes from *the way* words are said. Only a small amount of impact is transmitted via words' actual dictionary definitions.

Even if using measured words when dealing with a class, if the teacher is stressed, it has an affect on the students. In study of daily stress levels in a middle school, an interesting observation was made concerning student stress. Both students and teachers were asked to rank their feelings of stress on a scale of 1 to 10. The surprise? The stress level of the children on any given day correlated to the personal stress level of the teacher the day before (Sylwester, 2000). Through words and actions, we *do* affect our students. The emotional tone of an environment colors the context of an entire learning experience. So if a student enters a classroom on the first day of the school year announcing, "I'm gonna flunk this class. I hate English," it may be because the emotional memory, or the summary of past experiences with English classes, is negative. This student may be predisposed to a poor attitude toward the new class—and perhaps doom himself or herself to a similar negative outcome in the future.

There are practical steps that can be taken to avoid such predispositions to negativity. First, demonstrate genuine respect for students. Let the students see, hear, and feel energy and enthusiasm for the subject matter and the learning tasks and eliminate the traps that increase student failure.

RITUALS IN STONE

Anyone working with young people establishes rituals sooner or later, at least if they are survivors. Those who do not survive often fail because of behavior or academic management that falls short—it's too chaotic, too unfocused, or too scattered in approach. The start to the school year is a critical time to establish the ritual early and up front. Many teachers try to win over students immediately with engaging projects and enthralling lessons before students understand behavior expectations, grading standards, and classroom rules. A teacher is far more successful establishing clear, nonnegotiable procedures first and then providing exciting and engaging tasks within the parameters to serve as guidelines for student performance and behavior.

Yet current thinking steers educators away from organizing desks in rows or using lockstep teaching. Whereas a traditional classroom of 30 years ago defined ritual as "running a tight ship," our profession cannot center on simple classroom management and behavior control in a world that demands so much of our graduates! Clearly, our job is to maximize learning for every student. So if ritual is a key, its importance *must* extend beyond simply helping a teacher maintain his or her sanity and job.

Ritual, in fact, is needed by human brains to guide thought and action. It provides the safety and security for human brains to function in a learning environment. Although novelty and stimulation cause a brain to pay attention, novelty absent ritual is chaos. And although challenge is essential for growth and affective motivation, without ritual it produces uncertainty or reluctance. Human brains need "bearings" and seek to identify expectations so their behavior brings reward. Classroom rules are important, even those set arbitrarily by the teacher ("Line up at the back wall for recess" or "No one moves when the bell rings until there is silence and I say 'dismissed!'"), because then children know what to do, know what is expected of them, and hence what action to take for safe maneuvering. Following such clear ritual brings them acceptance and security. Whether it is the district, the school, the classroom teacher, or the students themselves who provide rituals, they lend certainty and safety to behavior guidelines (see Activity 2.1).

 Activity 2.1   Assignment Safety Check (ASC)

Purpose: To make certain that all students accurately record assignments.

Write assignments on a chalkboard or chart when they are given, as well as saying them aloud. That way, visual learners have an improved chance of getting the correct information. At the end of each day's work, institute a short ritual before dismissal. Ask students to get up and walk to another part of the room to cross-check with a classmate the accuracy of their respective recorded assignments for the following day. Bonus: Since students who are at risk are very often kinesthetic learners, this activity promotes movement with a positive purpose.

Students need to know that certain actions bring specified reactions in learning situations, as well—for example, that A leads to B or that wasting energy on option C is unproductive. Learners avoid "moving targets" because they create uncertainty and anxiety, hence the need for directness such as "Show me!" "Spell it out!" and "What can I do?" Nothing is more unsettling and discomforting than being unsure of the consequences of one's actions because no parameters for acceptable action have been defined.

As often as possible, provide exemplars, rubrics, or demonstrations to give students the "big picture." In each case, students will understand the features for a successful product—or view products and discover why they succeed or fall short in proving mastery. Rituals and established procedure make expectations clear. Activities 2.2 and 2.3 provide examples of this.

 Activity 2.2   Color Shape Markers

Purpose: To help students identify important information for study and review.

Instruct students to use consistent colors or simple symbols, as ritual, to mark specific types of key content in their handouts. Either colored pencils or crayons can be used to mark their material, as directed by the teacher. For instance, important dates might always be encircled with green, red boxes might be placed around new vocabulary, and blue can underline important facts for which they are responsible. Since the teacher knows the correct visual pattern when all items are appropriately marked, he or she can ascertain any misidentifications or omissions students make before the material goes home. This saves students from "escaping" from class without a handle on what is important for review.

This is a good ritual to share with parents on a back-to-school night, as well. Parents will understand that when a paper arrives home with a red box, a green circle, or a yellow underline, it signifies an important concept that must be learned by their child. They can help! Variation: If using a textbook that cannot be written or marked in, use transparent, removable 1/4" colored dots as substitutes for symbol and shape marks.

Figure 2.1   Text Markers

One of the greatest presidents of the nineteenth century was
Thomas Jefferson. Jefferson served after winning the (1800) presidential
election, and helped established the idea of the ⟨innate⟩ equality of all humans

---

 Activity 2.3   Dot Sorting

Purpose: To help students sort and organize large amounts of information in order to understand relationships.

Quarter-inch dots can also be used to color code important information. Each color signifies a particular classification, or rank, in sequence or importance. The teacher specifies color dots to mark main points: elaboration or supporting facts and subsets can be designated with another color. This activity can be an initial step in preparing students for outlining, helping students organize information from a text, or aiding student understanding of classifications.

Clearly, academic routines should be present in classrooms; any procedure, format, materials, or tools used consistently and routinely over time can qualify. Such academic routines can last an entire school year and pertain to only a single classroom, a whole grade level, or the entire school. If it is routine for students to use a consistent form or format, perhaps to make comparisons and contrasts, they will begin to organize the disorganized automatically. The revisited patterns, such as those evident in Activities 2.4 and 2.5, become visual memories, recallable when future needs arise for organizing ideas or relating concepts.

 Activity 2.4   Graphic Organizer for Comparisons (GO4C)

Purpose: To supply a tool to help students organize information in order to make a comparison between two concepts.

Figure 2.2   Comparison Organizer

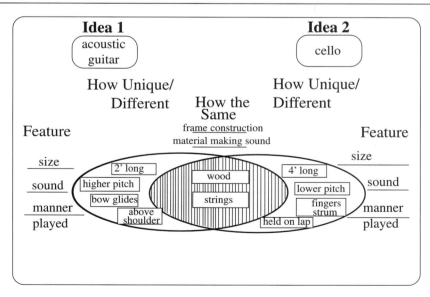

✳ **Activity 2.5**   Writing Dots
_____

Purpose: To provide a format for organizing information for writing projects.

Quarter-inch transparent dots, available at any office supply store, can serve as an inexpensive visual organizer for formula writing (common in state testing). Coated with light adhesive, they can be removed without causing damage to books. Teach students an organizational pattern of colors that remains consistent and unchanging throughout the school year(s). The pattern becomes a visual memory and template for an expository writing format.

1.   Learners can assess their own or a partner's essay by following these directions (*note: preinstruction on terminology and process is necessary*). Place one check mark in the left margin next to the first word of each paragraph. Count the check marks: There should be at least five.

2.   Look in the first paragraph. Place a red dot in the left margin next to the topic sentence. Read the final paragraph, and if there is a sentence that restates or says almost the same thing as the topic sentence, put a red dot in the left margin next to that sentence.

3.   Look in Paragraph 2. If there is a sentence that supports or elaborates on the topic sentence (primary support), place a green dot immediately next to it in the left margin. Repeat for Paragraphs 3 and 4.

4.   Go back to Paragraph 2. Read carefully and see if there are any details (second-level supports) to explain or elaborate on the primary support. Place a blue dot next to each and every detail you find. Repeat for Paragraphs 3 and 4.

5.   Compare the pattern of dots you have placed on the paper with the master pattern (see Figure 2.3) to measure success or shortcomings. A student can immediately tell what he or she is missing for a basic expository writing format!

Ritual exists in many forms, each important to human brains. It provides guidelines to operate in uncharted territory—where, after all, learning requires students to be. Expectations for behavior must be dependable and consistent so children know their targeted destination and can plan their journey. If students are assigned a writing project and told little more than to *be creative*, they sit and stare at the paper trying to

Figure 2.3   Visual Pattern for Expository Writing

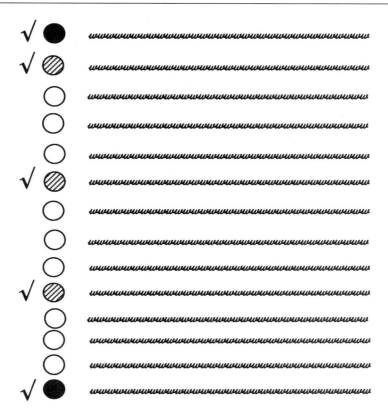

figure out what to do. Unmotivated students might begin to misbehave, and those highly motivated will fret, worry, and drive the teacher crazy with questions regarding directions to guide their work. But give students definite rules and guidelines, and they will take off—like birds in flight—following the pathways and direction established and using the imagination and creativity unique to them. They are safe! As George Smith Patton once remarked: "Never tell people how to do things. Tell them what to do and they will surprise you with their ingenuity" (1947, p. 357).

IDENTIFYING THE BIG PICTURE

Also necessary at the onset of any instructional task is identification of the *big picture*. It is a clear definition of the task or product expected. If you tackle a 500-piece jigsaw puzzle, do you dive right in or first look at the picture on the front of the box? If you were changing your first flat tire on a highway, would you read the manual verbiage only or first look at diagrams and read the steps afterward?

Students, too, must get a "big picture" before assembling knowledge or sequencing steps of a skill. It is like the man who takes his wife rafting down a West Virginia river, her first venture into outdoor sport. He gives her a paddle and, as soon as they encounter white water, begins shouting a rapid fire of orders: "Faster! No—on the left. Paddle on the right. Stop paddling! Left! Slower! Faster! Dig in!"

After successfully passing into calm waters, the wife lays the paddle down in the bottom of the raft. She curtly asks, "What were we trying to do?" The husband, fearful she was angry at his barrage of orders, tells her they were just trying to keep the raft in the middle of the river. With calm certainty, she responds, "If you would have told me that to start, I would have known what to do."

Indeed, she would have. For the big picture would have afforded her the ability to fill in detail to accomplish her ends through memory, connections, and problem solving (see Activity 2.6).

✳ **Activity 2.6**   Big Picture

Purpose: To help learners make connections and understand concepts by engaging related memory networks so that meaning is derived more easily from a task.

Before assigning material to children, preface the task with cues, background information, or a "big picture" to help them activate proper memory networks for understanding. Avoid assigning materials, such as the following paragraph, that are devoid of the big picture:

> With hocked gems financing him, our hero bravely defied all scornful laughter that tried to prevent his scheme. "Your eyes deceive," he had said. "An egg, not a table, correctly typifies this unexplored planet." Now three sturdy sisters sought proof. Forging along, sometimes through calm vastness, yet more often very turbulent peaks and valleys, days became weeks.

Confused? Had the teacher explained prior to assigning the passage that it was an excerpt from the diary of a man who accompanied Columbus on his first journey to the New World, it would have been much easier to comprehend the meaning of the passage.

CLASSROOM PROCEDURES

Finally, classroom procedure can contribute to a safe learning environment. School-age youngsters hold two common fears: the fear of failure and the fear of peer disapproval. Either can make students tentative about participating, as well as reticent about risk taking. As they grow older, children become ever more reluctant to take public risks that could end in failure or humiliation. According to Calvin Coolidge, "If you don't say anything, you won't be called on to repeat it" (Bartlett, 1980, p. 736).

Schools are places of learning. Learning requires change, yet change can be discomforting and risky. It is bad enough that school not only involves such risks, laden with potential failure as well as success, but it also features peers as an audience throughout the process. Even so, risks *have* to be taken to grow and learn. So how is the natural tendency to avoid risk taking overcome in learning situations?

Set Parameters to Measure Progress

First, definite directions, rules, standards, and parameters should be set to give students guidance in performing a skill or creating a product, because these will be used to measure student progress toward mastery and excellence. Students should understand that their product and performance are pitted against a clear standard—not against the subjective judgment of a teacher. Therefore, nothing is arbitrary, but instead, there are clear expectations and categories of performance. Students must be aware of that which they must master—and then, as in Activity 2.7, be given opportunity to prove it.

 Activity 2.7   Discovery Within Limits

Purpose: To invite students, at the onset of a new section of study, to follow guidelines to manipulate items, gain new understanding, and explain or prove their discovery.

Two to four students are given a container of items (including buttons, magnets, frozen treat sticks, cotton balls, paper, tin foil, paper clips, nails or brads, etc.) and directions like the following: "Inside this bag you will find a number of items, including magnets. You are each invited to use these or any other items within our classroom to make at least one important observation about magnets." Following their discovery period (perhaps 11–15 minutes), students should

(Continued)

Activity 2.7 (continued)

1. Return to their group and each share new ideas.

2. Answer each other's questions.

3. Be ready to report out group findings.

After the time has expired, debrief the entire class and record and compare their discoveries. Ask students to prove their discovery or ask them to provide extended questions, which should be recorded for reference later as unit instruction begins and answers or explanations unfold.

As an extension of such an activity, students could be asked to find how magnets are used in their own lives. They may note that magnets keep kitchen cupboards closed, serve as the core to motors that produce electricity, are a part of television remote controls, and so on. Now, book learning has some practicality, and there really *is* something in it for them. We may even be producing budding engineers, as the springboard to interest is information!

At times, choice should be afforded students about how to demonstrate mastery as long as predetermined guidelines or rules reflective of curriculum goals are followed. Doing so calls upon students to exercise creativity and stretch their abilities while honoring their learning preferences and still enabling them to hit the target (as in Activity 2.8). Students who are routinely asked to parrot back or duplicate a predetermined conclusion quickly learn that only replication is rewarded and the only context for using new information or skill is a test—hardly a motivator for learning. But if a teacher clearly identifies the desired goal, sets the rules for getting there, and lets 'em go, risk taking is encouraged (see Chapter 7).

※ **Activity 2.8   Double Check**

Purpose: To provide students with clear direction for information gathering and self-evaluation of the accuracy of predictions. Students make predictions based on prior knowledge, gather information, and argue a position.

Announce a general topic that students are about to study. Prior to reading unfamiliar material, such as a passage explaining meandering patterns of new rivers and erosion of embankments, have paired students read several brief statements that you have provided, all dealing with a new concept at hand. Examples include "A river's length can be expected to decrease over time" and "Old, established rivers are more likely to meander than newer waterways." Students will select the one(s) that they believe are true or with which they agree. Then ask the students to read the article, using their predictions as a reference. Ask them to use the text to either prove or disprove their prereading opinions, taking notes to either prove or refute their original opinions. Next, have the paired students discuss and come to consensus regarding their findings in the text and then turn in a written decision. Then randomly select one group's written decision paper and lead a whole-class discussion to compare and discuss the conclusions in the chosen paper. The entire class will then reach consensus as to the accurate information from the article.

Creating Safety for Participation

Robert Sylwester points out in *A Biological Brain in a Cultural Classroom*, "To create a chronically stressful school environment to increase learning is thus biologically both counterproductive and irresponsible" (2000, p. 41). Measures can be embedded in instruction to ensure safety and security for students, as well. If the goal truly is to maximize learning, all hurdles must be avoided that eliminate possibilities for active student participation in the business of learning. Instead, teachers must make risk taking and participation not only acceptable but also palatable to the student. Activities 2.9 through 2.16 provide a host of "safe" activities.

 Activity 2.9   Advance Preps

Purpose: To insure that students review and connect with key concepts in material prior to whole-class discussion, while improving the likelihood of student participation.

Preface the start of class discussions of homework with paired advance sharing by saying, "With your partner, identify the cause of the main character's failure to win the ball game in the story you read for homework" or "Check that you and your partner are in agreement with the surface area of the figure in problem 32." Such short, opening sessions can become rituals and should last no more than 2–4 minutes. In the short time, partners will check for comprehension, identify key points, clarify problem areas, agree on answers, and note common difficulties, all in preparation for whole-class conversation and sharing. Every student, even those who failed to do the assignment, will be

(Continued)

Activity 2.9 (continued)

exposed to material and become active in the task. Every student has some *contact with content,* increasing the likelihood that he or she can become a participant in class activities. This might be the best-spent time of the class period, especially if you want a class discussion that involves more than the same few, routinely eager students.

 Activity 2.10 Peer Teaching

Purpose: To force safe rehearsal and feedback in the midst of instruction.

In the midst of instruction, partner students and designate each as Person A or B. Designate a key concept for Person A to teach to Person B. Person B then tells Person A what he or she heard. Students can clear up misunderstandings, discuss concepts, and identify problem areas.

 Activity 2.11 Peer Pair Share

Purpose: To ensure that each student can generate answers/solutions to questions or posed problems with a high degree of safety.

Pair students following instruction for the purpose of answering questions or doing practice work for a concept. Student teams reach consensus in solving the problem. For example, a teacher might ask students to turn to a partner and agree on two major reasons why the lack of industry crippled the Confederacy's ability to win the American Civil War. Ideas are then shared with the entire class or group, lending confidence in the soundness of any jointly generated conclusion, while making it safer to voice joint concerns if there is uncertainty.

 Activity 2.12 Think Teams

Purpose: To use peers in a safe setting to share and coach students and to provide feedback.

Assign "think teams" comprising two to four students who are located near one another during classroom activities. The groups can remain stable for days or weeks or until seat assignment or room configuration changes. When a question is asked, a problem is posed, or practice of skills is needed, these teams jump into action to coach, share, reach consensus, and provide feedback to each other in the task. It is social as well as kinesthetic, provides a change of state, and is safe.

 Activity 2.13 Community Groups

Purpose: To provide a safe, secure environment for all children through peer support and membership in a small social community.

Form stable, unchanging base groups at the beginning of the school year or term. They should not be academic or formal instructional groupings; instead, these teacher-assigned groups record assignments and collect materials for absent group mates, phone each other during extended absences, conduct joint classroom duties, monitor each others' celebrations or personal problems, plus lend support in general to others within their group. Each student becomes a part of a small unit, creating a greater sense of belonging. The groups can meet at the beginning and end of each class day for brief periods or during any other designated time period. Note: This activity is especially important in classes containing many at-risk students or schools with high mobility rates, where new students have few opportunities to "fit in" (Marzano, Pickering, & Pollock, 2001).

 Activity 2.14 Summary and Safe Check

Purpose: To improve comprehension when introducing new material in written form, while producing the opportunity for safe reflection.

Pair students and give them 3–5 minutes of work time. Ask each to silently read a short section of text. Partner A verbally summarizes the information read, with her book closed. Partner B checks for accuracy, with his book open for reference. Partners alternate turns generating and answering questions related to the text, ensuring that facts are gleaned and ideas are reviewed. Whole-class or group discussion can then follow, with all students armed with information and facts to share.

Activity 2.15 Random Response

Purpose: To provide a safe environment in which all students are accountable for generating and sharing ideas.

During class discussion or while students are working on individual tasks, pose a question or dilemma, such as "In our story, Pat's mother was very angry that the butter she had softening on the counter was missing when she was ready to butter the toast. What might account for the disappearance of the butter left on the counter?" Then place students into groups of four. The designated team works to reach agreement on a response, making certain that every member is prepared to represent the group as a whole in giving the answer. Each student will replicate the answer, produce the product, or practice a response. The group counts off to assign numbers, or staples papers together as a group to represent an ordered sequence. Next, randomly choose a number from 1 to 4. When calling for a team answer, the paper with the corresponding number or the student who holds the selected number is responsible to answer on behalf of the entire group. Team members will be certain that they, as well as their teammates, are prepared for success. They are accountable for themselves and the entire group.

 Activity 2.16 Scripted Consensus

Purpose: To promote student participation in the classroom through safe generation of ideas and consensus building.

Provide wait time after prompting to allow students to jot responses on scraps of paper (no need for spelling checks, complete sentences, etc., as this is for the writer's eyes only). These recorded answers, whether written words or pictures, become scripts which free each student up to listen actively and respond to ideas of others, rather than continuously rehearsing their answers for fear they might be called on next. It becomes reasonable to ask students to summarize the idea of the student preceding them in discussion before sharing ideas of their own, perhaps beginning genuine discourse within the group. Ideas and reasoning of a student are easily recalled when the student holds a "script" and can afford to shift focus to others' ideas yet not lose track of his or her own when called upon to share in discussion. The likelihood of good discussion increases.

Include one more step to increase safety and guarantee improved participation: Before asking for the sharing of ideas, have students quickly turn to a neighbor and pool ideas, reaching consensus on the single best answer and *then* call for discussion. Everyone has an answer; it is unimportant who is its original source, because all interacted to arrive at it and no one fails. And peer approval? At least one other person agrees with each student, as the idea is reached through peer consensus. No hurdles are set for the hard-to-reach student, participation for all is made easy, and the two basic student fears are overcome.

Teaching techniques such as wait time (see Activity 2.16) avoid rapid-fire answers, which increase the likelihood of error, but the fear of producing an incorrect (or no) answer still exists. Thus, participation from the weaker students does not necessarily increase. Perhaps worst of all, the contributions of classmates in discussions often go unheard, because students concentrate on their line of reasoning and key points—in case they are the next to be called upon to answer. No one wants to appear unprepared and foolish when their train of thought is lost.

At times, the main cause of lack of participation is not student fear, but student unpreparedness. Because our purpose is to maximize learning for every student, it is natural to feel frustration when students come to class unprepared. Kicking a student out into the hall for not doing homework may set an example, but it does nothing to improve learning for the offending student (or to set a positive tone for the class). The activity described in Activity 2.17 can involve even the most disengaged student.

 Activity 2.17 Silent Exchange

Purpose: To cause students to connect to and reflect on material prior to the formal start of class.

Before opening the class up to discussion of assigned homework, have students pair with a classmate (or assign pairs), and then direct them to a specific task. Tasks might require that (a) students seek answers to questions posed and be ready to report out if called upon; (b) one student shares a discovery, concern, or key point with his or her partner, who verifies or answers the concern, using the text as a reference; or (c) Student A writes a question on paper and gives it to Student B, who then answers or responds, and then they switch roles. Note: This can be done effectively in a totally silent room, which is very effective for secondary-level students.

Learning is a tough journey that requires effort and growth. To ensure that each student can find the way, educators must set clear expectations within a solid framework. Yet through it all, there must be the soft touch of the positive to make each student a willing and active participant who is guided and encouraged—and not just a spectator forced along for the ride. It is about teaching *smart*.

3

First Get 'Em on the Line—Then You Can Reel 'Em In!

The initial cause of any action always lies in external sensory stimulation, because without this, thought is inconceivable.

—Ivan Mikhailovich Sechenov, 1829–1905

ENGAGING THE BRAIN

If the goal of educators is maximized learning for each student, the end result of teaching efforts must be successful planting of long-term, retrievable memory. We teach a content or skill not because it is important for sixth grade but because it is important for *life*.

Robert Sylwester (2000) has described the journey toward any behavior reflective of learning and long-term memory as a four-step sequence. Note that this straightforward pathway involving input → process → output or performance starts at a most basic point: novelty (see Figure 3.1). The brain chooses between sensory stimuli competing for notice to react to and process. Intrigue children with firsthand experiences such as those in Activities 3.1, 3.2, and 3.3.

Figure 3.1   Learning Sequence

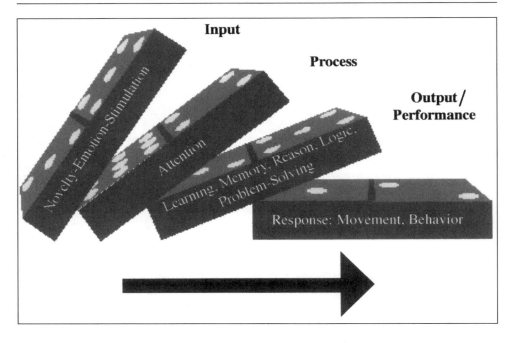

✳ **Activity 3.1**   Catch-Ums

Purpose: To capture student attention by allowing children to draw a personal connection to content.

Make learning come alive by telling stories about the lives, discoveries, trials, and adventures of real people. For instance, in beginning a study of the blustery Theodore Roosevelt, intrigue children with the story of his shyness and feelings of inadequacy by saying, "At first, he was afraid of everything. But he pretended not to be, until one day he discovered that he was no longer afraid." Such stories personalize historical figures.

Share the story of the origin of words to make them more memorable. For instance, the word *nightmare* is a compound of *night* and the Old English word *mare*, which refers to an evil spirit thought to afflict sleeping persons by sitting on them. Children are not apt to forget words taught in this way!

Activity 3.2   Sock It to Me

Purpose: To help pre-K to K children become more observant and learn to use all senses, not just vision, to gain information.

Demonstrate to children a guessing game. Secretly place an object in a fabric sack or old sock and then ask the children to try to guess what it is without looking inside. Since the children are unable to rely on sight, they will be forced to figure out how else they might discover what is inside. They will likely suggest feeling the shape of the object, holding it to determine its weight, smelling for odor, or shaking to hear if the object makes noise. Each will provide clues to help properly identify the mystery item. After all senses other than sight are used, reveal the object and let children evaluate the accuracy of the guesses.

 Activity 3.3   Quick Solve

Purpose: To provide novelty and stimulation that is initial and *ongoing* throughout an instructional task by engaging the brain, tapping into existing knowledge, establishing a practical demand for content, and providing the instruction needed to solve the authentic dilemma facing students.

- Tell (science) students, "The next-door neighbor wants to hire you to move a section of concrete that is cracked and needing to be replaced from the front sidewalk before new concrete can be poured. You gladly accept the job, since you earn spending money by doing odd jobs in the neighborhood. After you arrive, however, you find that the broken section is 3 × 4 feet, 110 pounds, and needs to be moved at least 3 feet out of the way! You are in sixth grade and not very strong. How would *you* complete the job?" The learning task progresses as follows:
- Students write down their ideas for solution on scrap paper and throw it into a hat (allow 1–2 minutes).
- Each student picks one piece of paper from the hat and considers the new idea and how it compliments or negates his or her own idea(s) (2 minutes).
- Students partner to formulate a solution to which they can both agree (2–2.5 minutes).

(continued)

Activity 3.3 (continued)

- The teacher debriefs the entire class, with students sharing ideas they have settled on as well as those from others that were rejected. Teams are expected to justify opinions (about 3 minutes).
- The teacher delivers instruction for 6–10 minutes on the concept and workings of a lever. Explanation, examples, and details are given.
- Youngsters write down key concepts and then turn to a neighbor to verify if their understandings are the same (1½ minutes).

Student questions or concerns are addressed in the whole class, followed by a reading assignment that explains the concept (text, most likely). Possibly homework questions or review or practice sheets might be assigned to lay groundwork for practice, elaborate upon the concept, or lay foundations for the following day's lesson. Note the variety, the fast pacing of the lesson, and the constant reengagement of the brain. The novelty and ongoing stimulation increase the likelihood of involvement and reduce the likelihood for apathy and boredom. The social interaction so enjoyed by young people is framed within rigid parameters set by a teacher in total control. The movement appeals to the kinesthetic learner, and participation is made safe through consensus building and anonymity. This is time well spent: The whole lesson takes a little over 20 minutes.

Incoming sensory information from both body and environment is continuously scanned by the human brain and then monitored for that which might be novel. It instantaneously sorts and filters incoming stimuli to determine and then act upon those to which it will attend. The preferences (a sight, a sound, a sensation) cause neurons essential to processing the chosen sensory input to fire in synchrony, creating brain circuits or communication networks. These brain circuits determine body and brain reactions—to drive behavior, enable thinking, and maybe even create physical movement. For example, when a reader spots that last word on a page in an exciting novel, he or she turns the page; a squirrel running onto the highway causes an automobile driver to swerve.

The same sequence of events occurs in a learning task within a schoolroom. To effectively lead students on the learning pathway, teachers must first grab attention. If none is paid, the subsequent milestones in planting memory will never be reached. No attention?—no activity. No activity?—no learning. This is because learning involves a reaction to sensory stimulation deemed important enough to attend to, followed by some action (behavior or movement) which demonstrates knowledge or skill. As in Activity 3.4, experience coupled with emotion produces mood (step one), which, when coupled with reason (step two), becomes thought. It is then that we arrive at step three, which is learning—ever more reason to get the first two steps right in the progression toward the fourth and last step, long-term memory. For without them, there will be no steps three and four.

 Activity 3.4   Circle Hop

Purpose: To create a practice session for playing notes efficiently and automatically on a flute whistle, using movement and novelty.

With each child instructed in use of a flute whistle, ask students to practice three chosen notes in unison as the teacher identifies them, such as B, A, and G. Place three circle hoops on the floor in a straight row (OOO), or taped squares in the same configuration (about 2 × 2 feet in size). As the class looks at the spaces from left to right, each will represents the three notes to be practiced, in order from highest to lowest, left to right as children view them. Instruct the class that a student leader will jump from space to space, and that they are to play the corresponding note on their flute as the leader's position changes. Rotate volunteers to serve as leaders, repeating the process. Any tune, any rhythm can result—providing a playful way of orchestrating practice of the new notes learned (adapted from the observed work of Sarah Dizney, a teacher in St. Johns County, Florida)!

Educators need not become classroom entertainers but rather must find ways to hook brains into *wanting* to learn. Sparking student interest in age-appropriate ways to reflect targeted content or skills is central to good teaching. The element of surprise makes learning take "hold" with greater ease; this was discovered in a functional magnetic resonance imaging study of causal learning. This matters even in correcting misperceptions with accurate information: According to *Nature* magazine, that which has already been learned ". . . can be revoked by the unexpected, and the element of surprise brings about a predictive of behavioral change." Activity 3.5 demonstrates the use of surprise to encourage learning (Waelti, Dickenson, & Schultz, 2001, pp. 43-48).

Activity 3.5   On the Line

Purpose: To help students understand notes "on the line" versus "in the space" in music class through a novel, memorable approach.

Use a frame with five strong twine strings spaced evenly and pulled tautly to represent the lines on a staff of music. Demonstrate how a note (represented by a tennis ball with a slit cut for a mouth and eyes and hair glue-gunned on tightly) can reside either *between* the lines (in spaces) or *on* the lines. To represent this concept, squeeze the tennis ball to open its "mouth," place the string inside, and release the ball. The ball will hook onto the line like teeth clamping onto a rope, and children will not forget the concept (adapted from the observed work of Sarah Dizney, a teacher in St. Johns County, Florida)!

Figure 3.2   On the Line

The desire to engage students in new material leads some teachers to begin a new unit of study with some fascinating (and often obscure) fact about the topic. Presented in isolation, it is meant to excite youngsters with intrigue and drama before introducing a chapter or delivering content. A better approach, however, encourages students to gain a handle on some basic concept, perhaps by discovering key information *before* formal instruction even begins. Such an approach can be a dynamite way to engage brains while creating curiosity about an upcoming topic (see Activity 3.6). People become interested in things about which they know a little something already—and want to discover more. If youngsters discover facts and gain know-how prior to formal instruction, their knowledge may become the catalyst for searching out additional information. As in Activity 3.7 it may become a springboard for learning!

 Activity 3.6   Entry Questions

Purpose: To intrigue children with a broad, encompassing question or prompt that is thoroughly answered through instruction.

When studying life of early settlers in the North American Great Plains in the 1850s, post a photo taken in the era. Use a picture with much detail, perhaps with a family dressed in period clothing seated in front of a sod house with domesticated animals, the prairie in the distance, and farm/home implements in full view. Post a question: "Where and when was this picture taken?" Perhaps also post photos or related pictures, mystery clues, or the like before introducing the topic. Then begin the unit of study with guesses, hypotheses, and solutions that can be verified or refuted through study and instruction.

 Activity 3.7   Examples to Concepts

Purpose: To have students use inductive reasoning to discover concepts through use of real-life examples prior to in-depth instruction on a topic.

At the beginning of a study of animal behavioral adaptations for survival, show students a video (or photos) of various creatures functioning in their natural environment. Perhaps include a peacock splaying his enormous tail feathers when confronting an enemy, a blowfish puffing himself to triple his size as he confronts a threat, an anaconda coiling around a rodent to suffocate it before ingesting the creature, or a cat bristling its fur as it encounters a dog. Instruct students beforehand to make as many observations as possible about how each animal has adapted to survival in its habitat. Students will begin to understand animal adaptations for survival by observing how a creature's size, shape, and physical characteristics serve its needs. Then, after debriefing and discussing, have students tackle a passage of text and find facts or explanations that can clarify or help organize their initial observations.

In addition to the novelty of its approach, personal discovery allows each student to explore in ways appropriate to his or her developmental stage and level of understanding or learning preferences. Plus, kids learn from each other when they speculate and explore. They question each other, share, and argue points in debrief sessions—and learning becomes *theirs*.

 Activity 3.8   Focus 1-2-3

Purpose: To use multimodal stimulation to hook student interest, leading students to understand how perspective, analysis, and weighing all the evidence are sophisticated elements of critical thinking.

Prior to class, set up an overhead projector so that when it is turned on, it will be totally out of focus. After class begins, project a transparency (out of focus) with lots of detail, such as a colorful work of art or a scanned photo. Ask the class to view the image and decide what it is. Guesses will be varied and interesting; allow children to share their ideas with a partner, within a group, or with the entire class and to justify their theories. Do not correct or comment on their accuracy, but instead ask children to watch the image as you focus it slightly. Do so, and have students decide whether their ideas have changed and, if so, why. Continue the gradual, incremental focusing until the image is completely in focus. There will be genuine surprise at what the image really is, as it is unlikely that anyone has the correct idea from the start. At this point, lead a discussion on (a) the importance of reserving judgment until all facts are in and (b) showing how differently we all perceive things (perspective).

A process like this can be used effectively to introduce a literary theme when teaching literature. It also works to introduce a social studies lesson on the need to gather *all* facts before generalizing or in art class to help students understand the effect of color and texture on visual impact.

Yet engaging a brain at the onset of a lesson is not enough. It is but the first of a repetitive process of engaging and *re*engaging the brain throughout an entire instruction process to enable students to make meaningful connections necessary for learning. A brain can be stimulated quickly on a snappy attention-getter but become distracted by another event immediately after. In a teaching–learning scenario, it is *sustained* involvement through extended periods of time that affords opportunities to

- Connect new information to established memory patterns
- Apply skills or manipulate ideas to become proficient
- Find practical application in one's own world

Maintaining focus on skills and concepts is integral to skillful teaching and for maintaining continuous participation throughout every learning activity. It is of little consolation to masterfully captivate a classroom of children only to lose their mental involvement within moments.

 Activity 3.9   Math Grids

Purpose: To help children understand the concept of "squaring" a number via engagement, manipulation, and practice throughout an entire learning task.

Demonstrate the doubling of numbers (adding a number to itself) through analogy or narration. You might show them a cone with a single scoop of ice cream and then talk about getting two scoops: Elicit from students that this is called a *double* scoop. Perhaps children could share other *doubles*, such as double duty, doubling up, and so on.

Then, begin a discovery phase. Explain that a double is what we call adding a digit to itself, but there is another name we give to a digit that results not from adding itself to itself but by multiplying it by itself. Announce that today the class will figure out what that name might be!

Demonstrate for students a visual process to understand squaring using an overhead with a projected grid. Represent a 1 unit × 1 unit grid and count one by one down the left side and one by one over the top side of the grid. Color in the field while students count the number of blocks (1) involved. Then announce that $1 \times 1 = 1$. Next, represent 2×2 by counting both down and over by two, and color in the resulting field. Students should count along to determine the number of blocks involved (4).

At this point, give students grid paper and crayons of their own, and ask them to try to produce a multiplication grid for 3×3, determining the number of blocks colored in. Ask students to turn to a neighbor to compare their results and answer each other's concerns, and then debrief the entire class by inviting a student volunteer or volunteer team to come up and demonstrate the idea on your overhead. Allow students to work in pairs to create additional multiplication squares up to 10, requiring each student to replicate the work (work and process are shared, products produced, and results recorded by each individual, with input from the partner). Each student records and creates the product individually.

(Continued)

Activity 3.9 (continued)

Next, debrief the entire class and ask what discoveries they have made—could they come up with any sensible name? Did they make any observations? Children will generate, and understand through involvement and ongoing manipulation, the concept of squaring. Record results for the entire class.

[Note: This is a great way to increase collaboration in problem solving and ensure social interaction. For the high-ability student, the progressive results can be noted and patterns discovered for graphing on a coordinate grid (1, 4, 9, 16, 25, etc.) or creation of a formula (sequenced intervals are 3, 5, 7, 9, etc.) to represent the progression of number squares (Lazenby, 1994; with special thanks to Johanna VonGeldern, Joseph Henry Elementary School, Galway, New York)].

Figure 3.3   Math Grids

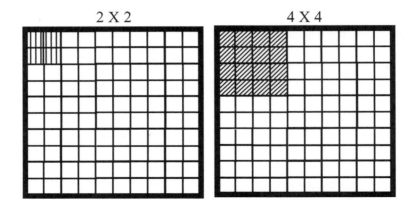

AVOIDING THE BRAIN BANE: MONOTONY

Caution: A captivating personality or skillful storytelling is not the stand-alone solution to gaining and maintaining attention and connection to content. It might be a good place to start, but too much of *any* "good thing" can be self-defeating. Every human brain has a common loathing—in or out of a classroom—and that is boredom and monotony. Brains constantly seek the stimulation and novelty in sensory information that warrant attention. It is the unexpected that captures and the new that intrigues: Sameness does neither. A person may sit politely through an ongoing speech and find himself or herself compiling a shopping list or thinking about picking up kids from soccer practice. A fan can wait 3 months to hear his or her favorite performer live but wish the concert was over after 50 minutes. Adults can attend a workshop and gladly become engaged in the first group task but after the fourth group activity in an hour might want to scream, *"Leave me alone!"* Ever put on your favorite CD at the start of a vacation road trip and then feel the urge to fling it out the window after the seventh time playing it? Have you ever been trapped in a room with an unpleasant odor only to discover that in time the odor was no longer evident, but when a new person entered the room, they commented on the smell?

In each case, your brain is doing what brains do well: focusing on and responding to stimulation that is novel. Once the stimulation repeats long enough, it becomes monotonous to the brain, and the brain tunes it out. It looks for new stimulation and relegates the monotonous stimuli to background as it brings the new information to the forefront of awareness. Quite literally, this happens in every life—too much work from the same talented artist might cause one to collect and purchase a new style of work; too much of the same brilliant music, too much noise, too much silence, too much talking, too much activity, and (gulp) even too much chocolate is simply too much of the same thing. Whew, that brain is brutal.

Young people are the same as adults in this regard. No matter how talented an instructor is in any one methodology, too much of the same sooner or later loses student attention. To keep focus, good instruction "shifts gears"—it is not all lecture, yet not all group work; not all silence and surely not all commotion. Move from pair sharing to group activity,

---

 Activity 3.10 Differentiated Discovery

Purpose: To provide a stimulating, novel way for students to gain understanding about electricity (via manipulation and discovery).

Place students in triads, inviting each to take a box with paraphernalia relating to information about electricity (for example, pieces of insulated and noninsulated wire, 1.5-volt batteries, 1.5-volt sockets and bulbs, a 1.5-volt motor, paper, and knife switches). Give the children the following directions: "Use any of the materials you want in this box to discover something that you did not know before." Because this task accommodates a wide range of abilities, each child will learn something appropriate to his or her developmental or experience level. Some children will feel the wire turn hot when it is connected to the bottom and top of the battery. Some may find a difference in the use of insulated versus noninsulated wire, others may light bulbs, some may find that bulbs light regardless of the way wires are connected to the battery(-ies). Some may set up series or parallel circuits, and some may even fashion a simple fan or propeller! Ask students to share their discoveries within the group, and then ask them to list three discoveries to share with the entire class. Debrief the class, chart the variety of discoveries, and allow them to serve as a foundation to build on or refute in upcoming lessons (adapted from Martin, 1997).

from a video clip to journal writing, and from lecture to whole-class discussion to seat work. Mix up the tasks.

Today's block schedules feature longer class periods, and therefore varied activity is critical but so, too, is it in 30- or 40-minute teaching segments. Students might survive monotonous activity for 90 minutes, but if they do it will be out of obedience or politeness. Their retention might be poor at best, because their thoughts will turn to personal thoughts, day-dreams, or other activities—and precious instructional time will have been wasted. Strive to change the state of the learner or the learning activity no less than every 15 to 20 minutes. Sustained attention is not a forte of human brains, especially when it comes to activities involving detail in monotonous environments. Thus much classroom work—solving a page of math problems or answering the questions at the back of the chapter—may be tough for children, as the brain finds vigilance to an ongoing, basically unchanging environment a difficult chore (Sylwester, 2000). Variety in approach and student tasks is important for learning (see Activity 3.10).

Changes of State

It is quite difficult to teach anything of substance to anyone in 15 minutes! But best practice does not dictate changing topics or concepts entirely, but rather *just changing the state or activity*. It can be done by moving to a different place in the classroom, altering the volume or pitch of your voice, or inserting pauses and silence into your speech to jolt brains to attention. Changes of state occur within the classroom when instruction is delivered for 10 minutes and the teacher pauses as students turn to a partner to repeat exactly what they heard. It occurs when students work for 15 minutes within a small group and then return to their seats to solve problems or work from the text. Follow that up with a handout that allows for reflection or application of material, and time will pass quickly. Students will manipulate information, and brains will remain focused. It works because brains are acquiring what they crave (novelty) and avoiding what they loathe (boredom and monotony). Sounds like win–win.

Providing changes of state through sequenced, reinforcing activities honors the full array of learning modalities. Educators have long known that traditional approaches to teaching favor the auditory and visual learners. Yet more often than not, students with language and behavior problems tend to be kinesthetic or tactile learners. If we want to reach all students and improve overall student achievement, then changing state and reengaging brains through variety in learning tasks serves the reluctant learner well. But it serves *all* children, because the longer any brain is engaged or reflective, the more likely it is to learn.

The Role of Movement

Perhaps one of the most important benefits of changing state is that we force movement: from passing out papers to raising hands; from speaking to writing to turning to a neighbor; from walking to a group setting to focusing eyes on a screen. Each time there is movement in a learning task, new regions of the brain become involved—the frontal lobe, the motor cortex, and the cerebellum. Thus, the number of brain regions activated in firing the memory trace increases, strengthening communication between brain regions. With more brain regions involved, the "ingredients" (nerve cells, or neurons) in the memory "recipe" (memory circuit) are greater in number.

Beyond change of state, honoring learning preferences, and multisensory input, there are yet other considerations for mindful use of movement in learning tasks. The basal ganglia and cerebellum, important brain regions for control of muscle movement, also help coordinate thought via connections with the frontal lobe (Hannaford, 1995) As David Sousa points out in *How the Brain Learns*, "There now is evidence that the cerebellum stimulates many more areas of the brain than previously thought, including those associated with cognitive function. Movement and learning have constant interplay" (2001, p. 231).

In addition, movement causes chemical changes in the brain that enhance learning. Deeply embedded in the midbrain region is the hippocampus, long known to be instrumental in planting and retrieving long-term declarative memory (for example, verbal and conscious facts, labels, category names, and locations). It is the center for long-term potentiation (LTP), often written up in journals and magazines, the process by which neural circuits become new or expanded memories. Neurons literally change physically and respond more strongly over weeks or years after active stimulation (Diamond & Hopson, 1998). Mindfulness of LTP is important in an environment that exists for the purpose of planting long-term memories—such as a classroom. Processes such as multiplying and dividing numbers, finding spelling patterns, investigating word meanings, and acquiring knowledge of the scientific method demand places in memory.

Brain nerve cells, or neurons, communicate via memory circuit electrochemically, with neurotransmitters (brain chemicals) central to the process. Neurotransmitters enable neurons to communicate and thus create the memory circuit. In the process of LTP for memory circuit establishment, one neurotransmitter is critically important to ". . . increase our ability to establish or reorganize neural networks so we may effectively think and remember" (Hannaford, 1995, p. 55). That is acetylcholine, one of several neurotransmitters released within the hippocampus. Among its several functions, it enhances the ability of the brain to perform LTP and, thus, to plant memories (Hannaford, 1995).

Now, this is key. Each time there is physical movement, acetylcholine is released in the brain to stimulate and attract new synaptic growth, increasing brain communication networks! So movement may actually enhance learning, not only for kinesthetic learners but for *all* learners. Keep an eye to movement's importance and encourage it in all tasks, and learning will be facilitated. Do not pass out the papers; have students retrieve them. Expect students to take notes, even if you are going to give them a word-by-word written account of an entire lecture. If a child with

Figure 3.4

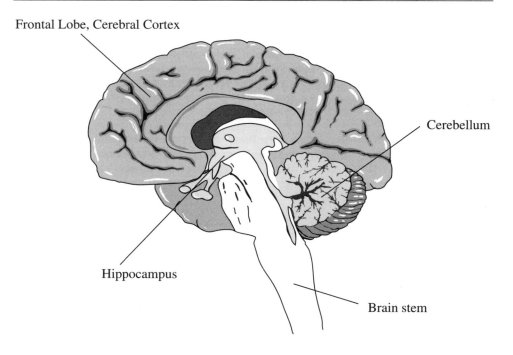

Frontal Lobe, Cerebral Cortex

Cerebellum

Hippocampus

Brain stem

a learning problem is unable to take complete notes, give him or her an outline to fill in. If necessary, give the student a fully detailed outline and have him or her circle words or underline phrases at your direction. Doing so involves more regions of the brain when planting the memory while the movement of the hand releases acetyolcholine to facilitate LTP. Provide opportunities for subtle movement, occasionally overt movement, and everything in between.

Varying Instruction to Facilitate the Planting and Recall of Memory

The likelihood of recalling a particular memory increases as that memory's communication networks become more extensive. The brain is amazing in that it does not need all neurons in the circuit restimulated to recall (or refire) the entire network. Just reactivating a small portion of neuronal columns of the many that make up a memory circuit causes the brain to scour its every combination containing that synchrony of neurons until it resonates on the correct full combination it seeks. Then, voila! A memory!

For example, one might have difficulty remembering a star's name when discussing a new movie. She might be able to describe hair color, facial features, or prior movies in which he starred—but not his name. Perhaps, after frustrating attempts at recall, she gives up and moves on to other conversation. Put it out of mind, right? Wrong! A part of the brain works subconsciously, behind the scenes, searching archived memories to hit on the correct combination and recreate the full memory. In the middle of grading papers 2 hours later, the actor's name, forgotten earlier, pops into her brain. Seems like a miracle.

Yet it is explainable. The more parts of the brain involved in planting a memory—from sound to sight to touch to smell to emotion to movement—the more ingredients (neurons) there are in that memory circuit. The greater the number of neurons involved, the greater the likelihood the brain will be exposed to enough stimuli to respark (recall) the entire memory. The more richly a memory is planted, therefore, the easier it is to retrieve. One is more likely to recall a memory that involves 300,000 neuronal columns firing simultaneously than one involving a network of, say, 200. Put simply, the odds are better for recall, as in an activity such as 3.10. Better, then, to plant a memory in a classroom through variety; not just through lecture or a text paragraph or a video, but all three. Better yet, use four or five ways (see Activities 3.11 and 3.12).

 Activity 3.11 Picture Story

Purpose: To involve multiple senses and processes in planting new memories or delivering new content.

To both ensure understanding and improve likelihood of recall for important vocabulary words, use narration and visuals. Assume the word *bower* is an important vocabulary word from an upcoming story. Using a felt board, a chart with colored markers, a white board, or markers on transparencies, quickly teach the word while telling a short story and drawing color scenes as it progresses:

> Tyrone arrived home early from school one afternoon. Walking into his kitchen, he surprised his mom, who had no idea that it was an early-release day. (Tyrone was not very good about bringing home notices from school.) She exclaimed, "Oh, Tyrone, I have to go into work and don't get off until 6 p.m. You'll have to stay in until I'm home."

(Continued)

Activity 3.11 (continued)

But it was a gorgeous spring day, so Tyrone pleaded with his mother to go out as long as he promised to be back before dinner. Because they lived in a safe town and Tyrone was trustworthy, his mother agreed. Off she went, and out went Tyrone.

He traveled up the lane, kicking stones the same way he had for years. Cutting across a field, he wandered back through high grass, listening to spring frogs and birds. A lush meadow off to his right caught his attention, and his curiosity led him to wander into it. An amazing sight met his eyes — there, to the north, was a dense stand of trees that seemed to stretch forever. He hurriedly scrambled to the edge of the forest. Peeking under the branches, he saw a shaded forest floor with no path and no evidence of others before him. He was amazed. The canopy was so thick that not a sparkle of light filtered through to the soft ground on which he walked. Suddenly, ahead, he saw dappled light and quickened his step. Then it happened!

The forest abruptly ended, and a clearing opened like a stage before him. Centered within it, a small building with a thatched roof stood. Simple, it had flower boxes beneath the windows—but no driveway, no road nearby, and no telephone wires. It was then that a creaking sound met his ears.

Tyrone stood in amazement as a small, hunched woman in a long, voluminous dress come out. She paused and looked, and, as she turned her hand, arose, with a finger pointing toward him. She said, "You—won't you come into my bower?"

Surely, the children will be intrigued. But there will be more. You can now ask what another word for *bower* might be. The students will have little trouble coming up with words such as *cottage, hut,* or *cabin.* But with prompting, the list can grow extremely long (especially when kids work in groups to produce *just two more words).* At this point, you can introduce the concept of synonyms (all these words mean similar, but not identical, things) and analogies: "A bower is to a person like a _____ is to a bird" and "A bower is to a person like a hive is to _____." Such a narrative approach could be the start to discovering more colorful vocabulary for creative writing, the way to combine a new word with imaginary story telling, or the start to a creative writing project.

The story can be told within a moment or two, but the importance of its approach is not speed, it is efficiency. The students are unlikely to *ever* forget the meaning of bower!

✳ Activity 3.12 Readraw

Purpose: To immerse students in a narrative through a variety of activities, involving a variety of senses, in order to improve comprehension.

Assign the reading of a story, followed by an oral reading (by either you or the students) of the same story. Next, assign each student a character from the story, whose identity they assume as they act out various parts or scenes of the story. Repeat the performance after assigning each student to a new character role. Then lead a full discussion with the class, asking them to identify the major scenes or events in the story and create labels to denote each. After the children place the event labels in the correct sequence, they will be put into small groups and asked to illustrate each scene. Upon completion, each group explains their artwork to classmates. Using the illustrations as a guide, each individual child writes the story in his or her own words. Not only does comprehension improve with this activity, but decoding skills also improve because children understand the story line more fully.

Catching the learner's attention early and often provides the incentive for varied instructional methods. The residual affect of such variety is multimodal instruction—and enhancement of learning for all.

4

Add It Up

The Whole Is Greater Than the Sum of Its Parts

The essential task of the teacher is to arrange the conditions of the learner's environment so that the processes of learning will be activated, supported, enhanced, and maintained.

—Robert Gagne, 1916–2002

COMPONENTS OF INSTRUCTIONAL ACTIVITIES

Novelty grabs attention, ritual sets the playing field, and challenge keeps brain skills honed for survival. All are important for learning and as such should be infused in planning and delivering instruction (Jensen, 1995). But it is important to look to the broad components of a learning scenario in addition to the characteristics of sound instruction. As Pat Wolfe (2001) points out in *Brain Matters*, we must select learning activities that provide what we want our students to gain rather than those that are chosen primarily because they are fun. Sound instruction must be driven by learning goals coupled with identified standards of mastery for all targeted content and skills. The study of the animal habitats might be founded on species adaptations for survival, with expectations that students can prove understanding of safeguards for species survival. The development of assessments aligned with targeted goals rounds out good planning and provides any educator the opportunity to deliver instruction effectively (Wiggins & McTighe, 1998). Within the planning and delivery sequence are broad components: content, process, and product. Each component, when scrutinized, reveals a defined and unique purpose within the learning scenario and is integral to learning itself.

Content

Traditional classrooms often focus on demonstration of mastery through formal assessment of content or prescribed application of knowledge and skills. There is generally a preconceived notion of the format, correct idea, manner of reasoning, or appearance of a finished product in learning and assessment. Replication and uniformity is rewarded. "The five reasons . . ." or "the three characteristics . . ." might define the correct response. In such an approach, duplication of content is the *end* rather than a *means* to the end: There is a commitment to a belief that a body of information and a prescribed application of skill provide the necessary tools to function in society. Information is static and defined.

Undeniably, some content is timeless and culturally essential. Language skills and basic math facts would fall into that category. Yet today's information explosion means much content is quickly obsolete, which makes its required commitment to long-term memory both futile and unproductive. Today's graduates might change professions two to three times over their lifetimes; yet each profession makes its own unique demands. Which skills to teach is an ongoing dilemma, and how long those skills will be current is the question. With fast-paced change, what role should straight content play in any learning discipline? To get a clearer picture, one must first examine the other two components of learning tasks.

Process

Classrooms must prepare children for *their* future world. Each career, each job requires skills and mastery of information peculiar to it. With each job change comes new challenges, requiring flexibility and transferable skills that transcend professions and enable workers to adapt to and function within a workplace. Critical thinking, accessing and manipulating information, synthesizing, communication, and social skills are among the essentials for such adaptability. As such, today's students must be exposed to learning environments that wire brains for such generic, transferable skills to empower them for strategizing, experimentation, problem solving, and production.

When mastery of a defined body of content is the primary goal, process involves "covering" skills or content—much like applying a coat of paint to a bare-wood fence. A learning task might begin with accessing prior knowledge and connecting it to a current topic of study—perhaps to entice students into learning. But lessons that center primarily on the transfer of content, which students are expected to replicate in a defined form, require application of that information in the context of a classroom—a worksheet, a quiz, a classroom response—not in the context of life. Students may recall well enough to earn a stellar grade on a test, but fail to realize connections and applications to their own world. The culmination? An assessment: You did it "right"; you earned the "A." You replicated perfectly—or not.

Children in content-driven classrooms study in order to *plant* memory rather than manipulate information for application and synthesis in the real world. A teacher may share *his or her* connections to the information, but instruction is often void of the opportunity for *children* to connect personally to it. Clear connections must be made between information or skills and a student's prior learning, current life concerns, and the real world around him or her, as in Activity 4.1. Educators who find themselves reteaching concepts that children failed to master in earlier grades must realize that humans tend to remember that which has importance for them (intrinsic motivation) and ignore that which has no meaning in their lives (see Activity 4.2).

✳ **Activity 4.1**   I Can See Clearly Now

Purpose: To help students gain understanding of abstract concepts or new vocabulary by (a) spotting similarities and making connections between unfamiliar concepts and understandings they already possess about their world and (b) connecting new concepts to their own lives.

When using a word or word root such as *penta* (or *aqua-, tele-, trans-, sept-,* etc.), expose students to a series of visuals representing the concept. For *penta-*, it might be drawings of a pentagon, pentagram, and a pentstemon, with students working in small groups deciding what characteristic they have in common.

Ask students to reach consensus about the feature through classroom discussion, and then lead them to discover that the common root *penta-* is a reference to that characteristic (having to do

(Continued)

Figure 4.1

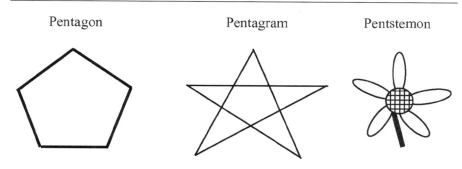

| Pentagon | Pentagram | Pentstemon |

with the number 5). Knowing that, ask students to predict—and then verify with a dictionary—the meaning of other words with similar roots (such as pentameter, pentose, pentomic, pentarchy, pentad, and pentathlon) before instructing them to check a dictionary for accuracy. Assign either the discovery of another existing word or the invention of a new word that accurately uses the root word *penta-* to reflect a related meaning. Then require them to draw or construct a representation of the new word.

Not only will the assignment allow for some creativity, it will also help reinforce the concept through manipulation of the meaning of the word root. Don't be surprised if they bring in more than one invented word—this can be contagious. The next day in class, each student can come forward and teach the new word!

If the word root has wide use, such as *tele-* or *trans-*, ask the children to discover any other words containing the same letter pattern in the newspaper, a magazine, or a favorite book, and watch their vocabulary grow. Remember: Language is about patterns, and if children begin to understand the syllabic patterns of words, they will begin to grow their vocabularies. Improved vocabularies are essential to comprehension.

 Activity 4.2   Circles

Purpose: To help children see a practical application for an abstract concept.

After introducing the concept of a shape, such as a circle, have students find examples of circles on graphic designs and in decorations. Follow that up with having children work in pairs to discover

(Continued)

Activity 4.2 (continued)

at least one use of the circle shape in the classroom or schoolyard that makes life either easier or more fun. Children may spot a merry-go-round, the side of a pencil sharpener, the bottom of a pencil holder, or the frame of a clock. Optional: Have children bring in an example or a drawing of something from their home that uses a circle andmakes their lives easier. Have children share and explain where the circle is on their chosen item.

Learning done rotely in a classroom using texts and workbooks and that demands memorization solely to earn a passing grade does little to promote student discovery or application. Real-life manipulation and adaptation *intertwines* memory networks to help learners make connections, comprehend nuances, see relationships, make contrasts, and detect similarities (see Activities 4.3, 4.4, and 4.5). The ability to compare, contrast, and understand relationships helps children predict outcomes and find solutions—in their *own* world. Empowerment! As Aristotle states: "For the things we have to learn before we can do them, we learn by doing them" (Bartlett's, 1983).

 Activity 4.3   All Over the Map

Purpose: To help students use map skills for problem solving and authentic tasks.

Have students follow the newspaper for a week, reading stories from different locations around the world. Using atlases, have students look up the latitude and longitude of the cities from where the news comes; locate the city on a large classroom map using the latitudinal and longitudinal information.

Ask students where, if they are the campaign advisor, they would schedule a state candidate to make campaign speeches to draw the largest audiences to hear their candidate. The candidate has only 7 days to travel, can make speeches only up to 5 hours per day, and is traveling by automobile. Have children work in groups of two to four and give them use of a regional map with population keys, a scale, road locations, and mileage charts. Any solution requires application of map skills, such as use of the map key and scale to solve authentic tasks. It is an open-ended task (more than one answer is possible) and entails choice, creativity, problem solving, synthesizing, and evaluation. Each group presents its proposal to the class, and each self-evaluates on the preestablished criteria (potential audience size, number of audience exposures, and travel efficiency).

✴ **Activity 4.4   Fulcruming Around**

Purpose: To use objects to discover a key concept and then find examples in the real world.

Distribute a ruler (balance beam) and a block to each pair of students, and provide a variety of small items of various weights (thread spools, coins, blocks, etc.). Teacher instruction is given to define the terms *balance beam* and *fulcrum*. Choose two different weights, and ask students to predict what might happen when weights are moved to opposite ends of the balance beam.

Figure 4.2

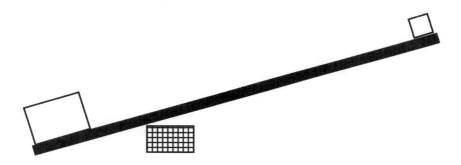

Next, have students test their predictions. Invite students to find a way to balance at least two different combinations of items, drawing the placement of items on the balance beam (ruler) once they are in complete balance. Students will then be asked to come to consensus regarding what they have observed. The teacher will lead a whole-class debrief toward the realization that relative weight and distance of objects from the fulcrum determine balance. Then ask students to find other examples of the use of a fulcrum in the world; likely, a teeter totter will be spotted on the playground!

 Activity 4.5   Now It's Your Turn

Purpose: To invite students to find examples of a newly introduced concept in the real world using creativity, goal setting, and humor.

After introducing a key term or concept (perhaps in science, language arts, or social studies), ask students to find examples of it— as many as they can—as a homework assignment. For instance, when

(Continued)

Activity 4.5 (continued)

running across the word *nocturnal* in a literary work, define and discuss the meaning from the context of the story. Then issue a challenge: Have them work for 3 minutes with two to three other people to generate a list of as many nocturnal concepts as they can. The sky is the limit: They can use dictionaries, textbooks, and class-room materials or be creative and do drawings. But the goal is to come up with 12 items that relate. When the target is reached, stretch them one step further by requesting 3 (or 5 or 7) more ideas when they return to class the next day! Many students will seek ideas from family members, and some will think of new concepts on their own. Give students 30 seconds to compare ideas with others at the start of the next class period before listing new additions in a whole-class debrief. The list will probably include everything from the following: bats, moon flowers, lemurs, cats, someone's teenage brother, and the tooth fairy! But certainly, the meaning of the concept will be cemented forever in memory. Time requirement? At most, 10 minutes over the course of 2 days.

It is difficult to motivate children when content has little meaning or application to their lives. Even if conscientious, a student who learns solely to satisfy behavioral demands (extrinsic motivation) forgets new concepts quickly when the extrinsic motivator is not present. So students might master science facts and score a perfect 100% on the final test only to revert back to inaccurate, informal perceptions a week later. If they mastered information short term primarily to perform satisfactorily on a test, they might never have reason to weave the information into their lives for practical use. They did not truly *learn*, they repeated (see Activity 4.6).

 Activity 4.6   Shape Museum and Shape Art

Purpose: To have students identify various basic shapes in functional products from their world.

After introducing various shapes (e.g., trapezoids, circles, squares, and right angles) to the class, ask students to bring in from home examples of those shapes to categorize and create a "shape museum," which can be added to as the year (or unit) progresses.

Provide students with photographs, postcards, or drawings of cities or architectural parts. Ask them to study the pictures and find any shape(s) embedded in them, including a circle on a scrolled ionic column, a triangle in the support of a staircase, and the rectangular outline of a skyscraper. Whichever shapes they spot, they must then outline or draw them and reproduce the shape in some original way, perhaps to create a work of art, design their own structure, or illustrate a story. (Imagine *Charlotte's Web* illustrated with only circles!)

Ideally, learning experiences begin with the teacher providing a "big picture." Explanations, rubrics, or exemplars give students a clear expectation for work ahead. Information is acquired on a need-to-know basis to make possible the completion of an assigned task. Then, students learn and practice skills in authentic, real-life tasks to test and prove mastery of learning.

The process of accessing, applying, and manipulating is an *extended stage* in facilitated learning, because it is here that the brain not only understands its task, but fills in details to accomplish it. If student realize they need specific content or a skill to solve a dilemma as in Activity 4.7, there will be reason to learn it to complete the task. They will practice strategies to prove mastery or complete a product. The learning activity is not centered on repeating back content from rote memory, but gaining new ideas and abilities *on the road toward creating a product* or finishing a task (e.g., writing an essay, giving a speech, passing a test, solving a math problem, performing a dance, or playing a sport).

 Activity 4.7   Menu Math and Catalog Counting

Purpose: To help students apply and manipulate basic math skills in real-world, "What's in it for me?" tasks.

1. Make up a typical menu from a restaurant, or ask a local eating establishment to supply copies of menus with extensive selections for meals. Rather than asking students to do 10 practice problems in addition at the end of a math chapter, hand each student one of the menus and these instructions: "You are out on a shopping trip with members of your family. Your mother has one more item to pick up at a store, so she sends you ahead to the mall restaurant to purchase lunch for your brother, your mother, and yourself. You have a ten-dollar bill in your hand and nothing more; what will your order be?"

(Continued)

Activity 4.7 (continued)

After completing this task, students can work in pairs or groups of three to double-check the accuracy of their math.

2. Ask friends, parents, and neighbors to save up the many holiday catalogs that arrive through the mail. Use them in math real-life tasks to force practice in application of basic math, as well as problem solving. Give students access to a wide variety of catalogs and ample time to complete the following task: Using any combination of catalogs, shop to buy a holiday gift for each member of your family. You must stay on a budget, because you have no one from whom you can borrow money. When you open your piggy bank, you find that you can spend up to thirteen dollars for each gift. You do not have to spend the same amount on each person, however. What will you buy?

List the page number of each gift, the recipient of each gift, and its price. Correctly add the cost of all items, and show how your choices allow you to remain within your budget.

Content serves as the means to the end. How it is used causes the brain to grow new connections—new synapses—beyond the standard ones already in existence. New meaning is gained (as in Activity 4.8), new relationships come into focus, new categories are formed, and memory networks are joined during the process segment. It is here that children strategize, take risks, fail or succeed, fine-tune and hone efforts, plan and test, categorize and combine, and create and problem solve.

The result? Not new ideas, but new ways to look at concepts, new combinations. Improvisation: higher level thinking! Process is a *pathway*, a course that uses content and skills (some new, some simply recombined)

✳ **Activity 4.8**   Tough Talk

Purpose: To expose students to complex social and political concepts through literature, language, and art.

Introduce a story with an important political or social theme, such as "Harrison Bergeron," by Kurt Vonnegut, Jr. The story examines a futuristic society in which the government places artificial handicaps on citizens to ensure that no one is superior to others, either physically or intellectually, contrasting mandatory equality with the struggle for excellence and expression.

The stage can be set through small-group discussion of a prompt provided by the teacher such as the following: "Is total equality between people the ideal for human society?" After giving students ample time to discuss the topic, facilitate the discussion, recording comments and ideas shared by the groups. Set aside comments and make no evaluation of points, even though there might be substantial disagreement between students.

Introduce the story at this point, explaining that it is set in the future, in a society where equality is a linchpin. Ask them to read the story, reflecting upon the original teacher question as they do ("Is total equality between people the ideal?").

Follow the silent individual reading with a small-group discussion session of the original prompt, and then open discussion to the entire class. Compare and contrast postreading opinions to charted pre-reading ideas. Strike a contrast between guaranteed equality versus guaranteed equality of opportunity.

Possible student observations and projects might include the definition of a theme or minor themes; the creation of editorial cartoons to express learned concepts; or debate, dance, theater, creative writing, persuasive writing, or Socratic seminars.

to progress from a task assignment to completion of a product which demonstrates the progress of learning—or proves mastery.

Frameworks for Performance Tasks

In orchestrating performance-learning tasks, a defined framework must be provided. Students can have no doubt as to what mastery entails. The qualities and requirements for the product assigned—whether tangible or intangible—are fully understood. Students are given a specific time period for completing the work, as well as requirements and rules that govern completion of the product. As in Activity 4.9, the product can take any form the student chooses, as long as mandated guidelines are followed to demonstrate mastery of the targeted skills and content.

Activity 4.9 Parachute Math

Purpose: To require manipulation of information and skill practice in an exciting learning task that intrinsically motivates students.

(Continued)

Activity 4.9 (continued)

Engage students in a parachute-making contest to help them master geometry skills, such as figuring surface area. Explain the task: to make a parachute that has the longest possible hang time and the smallest surface area. Using plastic from trash bags for the parachute, string for the tow line, and a paperclip as the skydiver, students experiment with shapes and dimensions. They will calculate surface areas of rectangles, triangles, circles and even heart shapes to find a solution to the task requirement. Some might make double-decker parachutes, and some may even design parachutes with the tow line off to one side to alter the descent angle. Combinations will abound as work proceeds to increase hang time.

As students launch parachutes, use a stopwatch to measure the time it takes for the parachute to land, carefully noting each descent. Have them graph their results on a coordinate grid (x = hang time and y = surface area). They will discover which portion of the grid is the more successful region and have fun while learning concepts in both geometry and graphing.

SOURCE: "Recalculating Middle School Math," Mann, L. (2000, January). *Education Update, 42*(1), p. 2. © 2000 by the Association for Supervision and Curriculum Development. Reprinted with permission from ASCD. All rights reserved.

Note that the task assigned demands progress toward mastery as defined through rules reflective of grade-level curriculum requirements for the subject being taught. Perhaps these are drawn from state standards, benchmarks, or school district mandates. But they are *not* negotiable, because there is accountability on the part of educators that students master them. *They* form the framework for the accomplishment of an assigned task in the form of expectations or guidelines toward the accomplishment of some product or demonstration. These can be content-based or skill-based, but they are essentials. Assessment of the final product is based on evidence of mastery of these standards (content/skills) via a pen-and-pencil summative assessment, evaluation of a rubric, a performance rating, or a combination of methods.

The process, or "work stage," of an effective learning scenario is multifaceted. It is here that instruction, manipulation, and *real* learning occurs. Students must strategize to determine a way to meet all teacher demands in order to produce the assigned product. There will be a need for information (obtained through research skills or practice of skills already mastered and building and reinforcing earlier learning), instruction from the teacher, and information acquired from primary and secondary sources other than the teacher. Inherent in the process will be

- Generation of new ideas
- Creative, divergent thinking to determine what is needed to accomplish the task
- Student effort to acquire knowledge and skill
- Organization and assembly of information/skill pieces
- Manifestation of work in a desired product, displaying evidence of mastery

Product: Defined and Purposeful

Students, in such performance tasks, will go well beyond the lower-level thinking skills of Bloom's Taxonomy, Cognitive Domain[1]—far beyond simple application. They are required to access and analyze information and then determine what is applicable to the dilemma (assignment) at hand. All elements are combined (synthesized) into a product appropriate to an attempted solution. The manifestation of all this work is the *product,* which is viewed in its totality to evaluate whether the criteria set in the initial teacher-mandated rules have been met. The student in the process stage performs at each level of Bloom's Taxonomy to create a product using content as a vehicle. This is evidenced in Activity 4.10.

 Activity 4.10 Birds, Beaks, and Habitats

Purpose: To have students demonstrate an understanding of how birds adapt to an environment for survival.

Provide background information regarding differing physical features of birds by viewing photos, videos, drawings, and books. Have students speculate briefly as to the use of different bird parts and how the shape or configuration of each might help the animal better adapt to its environment. Students will record in a sketchbook general categories of bird bodies, necks, heads, beaks, tails, legs, and feet.

Next, demonstrate bird habitats through simple simulations. A wetland is represented by a pail with shallow water and surface-floating objects. A pond is a pail with deep water and raisins or other nonfloating objects on the bottom. The forest food source can be a log containing holes stuffed with rice, representing insects in fallen timber, while the prairie is simply sunflower seed spread on a table top.

Next, show children pictures of real birds feeding in their natural habitats. Perhaps show woodpeckers, with beaks that operate much like tweezers to extract and eat insects in trees. Their long and sharp bill allows hammering into tree trunks, while still tail feathers help

(Continued)

Activity 4.10 (continued)

the bird remain upright while working. The long tongue, needed to help the bird extract insects, wraps around inside of the skull, while the barbed tongue helps the bird pull insects out from the tree. Two toes each face upward and downward to stabilize woodpeckers on the tree as they balance vertically to feed.

Provide similar detail for other birds: sparrows and seed eaters have heavy conical bills to split seeds open, and grosbeaks flock because seeds are concentrated in weed patches in open fields. Ducks and spoonbills eat aquatic vegetation near the surface, their fluted bill strains food from water much like a slotted spoon drains noodles, and their webbed feet propel them through water and help them walk on mud. Short legs located far back on their body help them swim efficiently, in contrast to geese, which have larger necks and longer legs to enable land grazing. Body parts are adapted to behavior.

This portion of the lesson can be quite exciting for children, because it's full of discovery and revelation. Children can speculate and hypothesize, analyze and marvel. Children may, at this point, try "feeding" in each of the habitats with tools that simulate beaks (tweezers, scoops, spoons, tongs, etc.) to experience the efficiency or frustration of each in distinct habitats.

For a performance task, have students create an imaginary bird by combining features from the seven characteristic categories introduced earlier and in direct instruction. Each category (above) contains multiple variations, so the combination possibilities are extensive. Children must "design" a bird with a particular habitat in mind: a wetland, marsh, prairie, forest, or pond. Students are assessed on whether the attributes of the designed bird ensure chances for successful survival in the chosen habitat.

The task demands manipulation of content, invites choice and creativity, requires synthesis, and invites self-evaluation—all parts of a sound lesson!

SOURCE: Ruth Wellman, Birchview Elementary School, Minnesota District 284. Adapted from materials provided by U.S. Fish & Wildlife Services, Minnesota Valley National Wildlife Refuge.

Notice the higher level skills built into this task. Analysis of body types, beak form, and feet confirmation generates possibilities for an invented creature. Strategizing leads to synthesis of a logical "new" species and then self-evaluation to measure progress en route to mastery or understanding. The process invites experimentation, trial, tweaking, and some final product. Yet a final product serves a unique purpose beyond the culmination of a task or proof of progress toward mastery. It is tangible evidence of a personal accomplishment. Accomplishment gives rise to feelings of self-worth: Product grows self-esteem.

CHOICE AND ITS BENEFITS

Important results of the process segment of a performance learning activity, then, include new products which reflect novel combinations of content or skill. Such tasks invite multiple solutions to academic assignments that, by necessity, demand that students make choices on their journey to completing an assignment. Choice is foundational to *any* creative process and surely to those that involve strategizing and divergent thinking. Brains react to choice with increased cognitive processing in the frontal lobes of the cerebral cortex as well as in the emotional centers of the brain, perhaps even increasing positive brain activity. Problem-solving ability improves, because its exercise sculpts the brain through formation of connections, enhancing proper communication of appropriate networks. Yet choice can also serve as an intrinsic motivator, because self-selection of avenues for processing reflects the emotional and attentional preferences of the person(s) involved (Jensen, 1996). Such bonuses for learning in the classroom!

FOUNDATION FOR GROWING A BRAIN

Choice, then, is a springboard for the brain's creativity to enable problem solving and divergent thinking when challenged by limited time or resources. Creativity requires more than simple imagination; it requires knowledge plus judgment based on teacher-/student-generated criteria. The brain goes beyond standard neural connections when functioning creatively to form new connections and intertwine memory networks in order to comprehend and solve. Note that such learning tasks require *inventive thinking*, not just replication or repetition. Accessing content, thinking with content, and creating with content is a skill combination of the future.

A word of caution: Remember, sound learning environments do not give students free rein, unbridled and uncontrolled. Choices are given *within rigid parameters.* These rules that set parameters corral kids into learning and practicing skills or content driven by standards, curriculum/district requirements, and grade-level expectations. Children are invited to accomplish a task in a variety of ways, because the task is open-ended, invites risk, and prizes novel expression—within the parameters of the framework (rules and criteria). Multiple intelligences and modality preferences are honored and made possible through a hallmark of a challenging classroom: *choice.*

NOTE

1   Bloom's Taxonomy, Cognitive Domain (Bloom, 1956), from the lowest to highest levels of thinking, includes the following: knowledge, comprehension, application, analysis, synthesis, and evaluation.

5

Paint Me a Picture, Show Me the Way

Reconciling the New With the Known

From the time one draws a first breath to the time one dies, the brain tries to make sense of its world, to gain an ever more accurate "big picture." Such understanding gives a person a sense of security to maneuver safely in his or her environment.

So how do we help students sharpen their pictures? Making connections for learning can be done in a multitude of ways, from verbal explanations to alternative representations to structured templates and visual organizers. Students might better understand new concepts through these clarifying experiences to reconcile the new with the known.

CONNECTIONS FOR UNDERSTANDING

Connections create understanding, as the mind sees underlying patterns and similarities between events or concepts that might appear on the surface to be markedly different. A student better understands how crocodiles move efficiently through mud when shown the similarity of the amphibian's skin surface to the tread of an automobile tire. An Ohio youngster can more accurately draw the general outline of United States when it is compared to a stretched outline of her home state. Identifying a sassafras leaf is easier when its shape is compared to that of the mitten-shaped state of Michigan, where it thrives.

> Maneuvering in a world of new experiences is made possible by spotting such patterns: perceiving distinct features, classifying those features, and making connections or contrasts between the new and the familiar. Taking botany classes on Louisiana flora gives one general insight into caring for all plants, whether they are grown in Baton Rouge or Portland, Oregon. As the brain acquires this ever-deepening pool of experiential memories, detection of repeating patterns helps the brain reconcile the world. At times, people are said to "fly by the seat of their pants," which implies extrapolating truths from earlier experiences and applying them to new situations. If one already knows how to play badminton, it will be easier to learn the rules of tennis; soccer, it will be easier to master hockey.
>
> Behaving in unfamiliar situations is made less risky when relying on old behavior patterns in some new combination to guide actions in dealing with new dilemmas. Patterns of sensorimotor activity categorize the world in terms of possible behaviors. This means cognition and behavior are not always driven by stimulus in a reflexive way, but are based on expectations arising from previous experience and stored as memory networks. (Engel, Fries, & Singer, 2001, p. 706)

Activity 5.1 demonstrates this.

 Activity 5.1   Math Patterning

Purpose: To help students discover patterns for solving new mathematical dilemmas by borrowing from previous experience.

Demonstrate to students that transforming a rectangle into a parallelogram by altering the figure angles does not change the formula for finding area, even though the shape of the object appears very different (for full discussion of the concept, see Bruer, 1999).

Cut a right triangular shape off one side of a rectangle, and place it on the other opposite side as students follow the same procedure. Follow the discovery process of Figure 5.1.

Figure 5.1

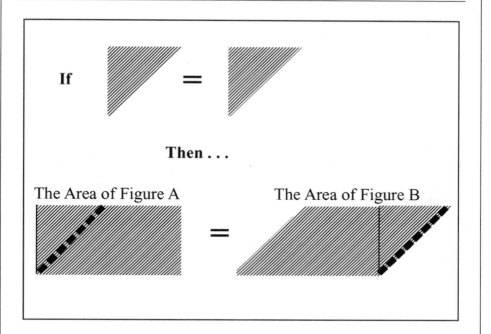

As a consequence of this discovery a behavior strategy might be employed for problem solving when a student comes across a question on how to find the area of a most unusual shape. If, indeed, one can remove a section from one portion of a figure and attach that exact shape to the remaining figure, the area of the figure as a whole will not change. Detecting similarities and patterns yields strategies for possible successful behavior. Transferable strategies empower children for maneuvering in their world. Note: This is a good segue into tessellations and can become an interdisciplinary approach to art.

Experiences such as these deepen the pool of tools available for problem solving and higher-level thinking so that when a person faces a dilemma he or she can tap into a long list of generic, transferable strategies. Recognizing features, drawing comparisons, and forming categories based on similarities and differences along both categorical and functional similarity are important skills for successful intelligence in life (Sternberg, 1996). As the brain detects patterns, the mind's picture of the world sharpens. And when the world is in focus, the person can operate with confidence. A Chevrolet owner can rent a Toyota while on vacation and drive with no difficulty. Patterns.

Figure 5.2   Patterning

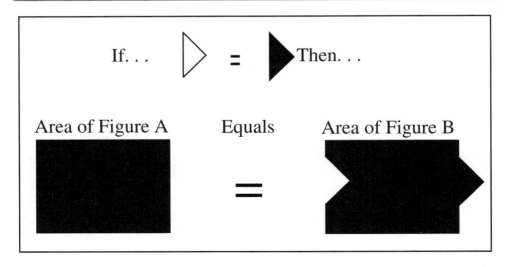

COMPARISONS AND CONTRASTS, METAPHORS AND ANALOGIES

There are ways to help a student better spot patterns and make connections. One particularly useful framework is a graphic organizer, used repeatedly and in the same format over a period of time. Each framework serves as a template to help children organize scattered bodies of information or sort out ideas and concepts.

Robert Sternberg, in *Successful Intelligence* (1996), identifies comparing, contrasting, and evaluating as essential to analytical thinking. The sophistication of concepts can change, but the same tried-and-true organizer may still work to detect patterns and make connections in K-8 (as with the comparison–contrast template from Swartz & Parks, 1994).

Such a form might be used to compare prose to poetry, Martin Luther King, Jr. to Mahatma Gandhi, multiplication to division, mammals to reptiles, or poetry to prose.

CHUNKING

Humans have limited memory space to manipulate and hold symbols at any given time. The number of symbols can vary from roughly two to seven for school-age children, which can be a stumbling block to the learner who is faced with working with significant numbers of symbols. In

Figure 5.3 Web Organizer

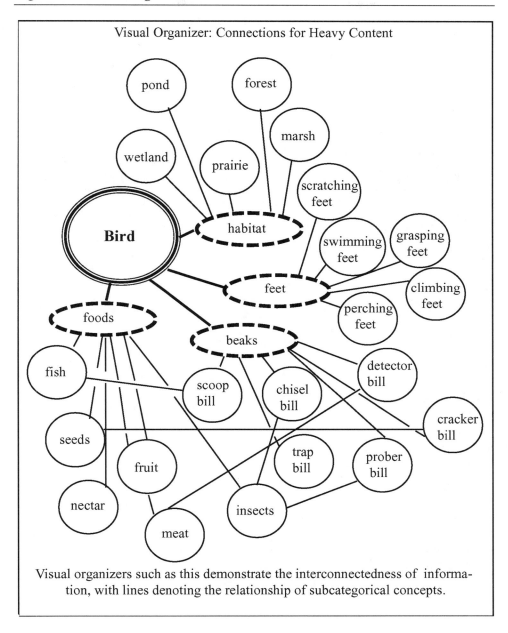

Visual Organizer: Connections for Heavy Content

Visual organizers such as this demonstrate the interconnectedness of information, with lines denoting the relationship of subcategorical concepts.

fact, when a first-grader struggles to sound out a new word, all available memory space may be devoted to decoding. So once a child completes the sounding out of the word, make him or her go back and reread the entire sentence, because, in the struggle to decode, the brain lost all understanding of what preceded the new word.

Figure 5.4   Organizer: Similarities and Differences

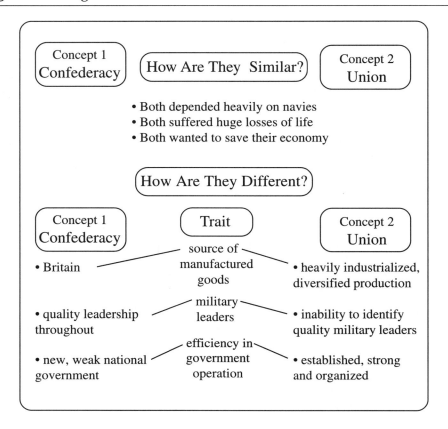

Memory space limitations affect more than just reading comprehension. Students are routinely asked to memorize and work with more than seven symbols as with numbers, lists, sequenced steps, and the like. Although some humans have an uncanny ability to memorize and recall information, it is because they have mastered skills for facilitating both. As skills, they are teachable (see Activity 5.2).

 Activity 5.2   Memory Strategies

Purpose: To instruct students in the memory strategy of chunking to facilitate recall of large volumes of information.

Share with students a lengthy (20 or more) list of unrelated items. Allow them 3–5 minutes to commit the list to memory and then lead a discussion to note the difficulty (impossibility) most experience in completing the task.

Next, demonstrate for students the technique of chunking: first, through formation of categories. Ask students to find two items from the list that seem to "go together," and then ask *why* they go together (thus determining the qualifying feature shared by members of the category) and if any other items from the list also could be in that chunk. After all items are categorized and students feel comfortable with their organization of items (see Figure 5.5B), have students then try to recall all items from memory by using the identified categories and the demonstrated strategy.

Invite other ways of grouping, categorizing, or *chunking*. Some students may create separate visuals for word combinations, and some may create a single narrative with concepts embedded within. Explain to students *why* the strategy works (the mind forms connections to help make sense of what otherwise seems disjointed information) and when it will work (whenever large amounts of content must be committed to memory for ready recall). A good source for more information on chunking is David A. Sousa's (2001) *How the Brain Learns*.

Allowing students personal choice in chunking methods and then providing them with practice opportunities will help children improve recall. Use of a chunking strategy in regular school work will increase the likelihood of automaticity in its application, which will help to forever deepen the pool of metacognitive strategies for students. Informed instruction demonstrates the strategy, and allowing students to practice helps them master it, but to ensure that children are empowered, do the following:

- Tell students *why* it works and *when* to use it
- Give immediate and ongoing feedback regarding progress

Children will use a strategy spontaneously and transfer it to new situations if they understand why it works and when it can help them learn (Bruer, 1999).

Chunking can be accomplished in ways beyond formation of categories. "E-n-c . . . y-c . . . l-o . . . p-e-d-i-a . . . ." After hearing this sequence, a flood of words and memories usually follows, especially if one is over 40 years of age. Songs! Once the sequence of notes, rhythms, and words begins to unfold, the brain will likely recall the remainder of the song easily. It can be quite a contrast to the amount of effort required to recite a list of facts solidly

Figure 5.5   Chunking

<table>
<tr><td colspan="5" align="center">**Memory Strategy**
Chunking - Categorizing</td></tr>
</table>

A.

Helicopter	**Oak Tree**	**Buzzard**	**Ship**	**Television**
Wrench	**Bicycle**	**Magazine**	**Tulip**	**Pelican**
Touch	**Dove**	**Fern**	**Hammer**	**Newspaper**
Screwdriver	**Robin**	**Radio**	**Yew**	**Plane**

Chunking categorizes informational symbols by feature, via similarities shared by all members of the chunk. Each "chunk" then functions as a single entity within the brain, which when "opened" operates like a file folder: full of items that share some commonality.

B.

Birds	Plants	Means of Transportation	Tools	Means of Communication
Dove **Robin** **Buzzard** **Pelican**	**Oak Tree** **Tulip** **Fern** **Begonia** **Yew**	**Helicopter** **Bicycle** **Ship** **Plane**	**Screwdriver** **Wrench** **Hammer**	**Touch** **Television** **Magazine** **Newspaper** **Radio**

The use of metacognitive skills such as this can empower students to become more effective learners. Allow for repeated, consistent use of such a method, to enable students to commit the process to long-term memory, to become a tool that can be applied to life situations whenever appropriate. The basis upon which categories are formed can be many and varied, according to the personal and attentional characteristics of the person doing the chunking. The *process* of chunking is of importance—not the formula for creation of categories.

---

memorized years before. That can entail much hard work and perhaps even be impossible. But memorize lyrics to a favorite song? Piece of cake: "Chantilly ___ and a pretty ___ . . ." (please see Activity 5.3).

The brain comprehends meaning with greater ease from pictures and icons than from individual ideas or symbols. The latter are perceived singly and then connected and reassembled for understanding. Contrast, for instance, the amount of effort required to process one icon that represents a windshield wiper on a car control (perceived as a single visual entity) versus the effort to read and comprehend 15 letters that must be combined into two separate words to be understood. And stories? Like music, they unfold sequentially. Fact A links with Fact B, which in turn links with Fact C. So when expecting students to memorize key facts about the Battle of Gettysburg, tell them first the story of the battle. This enables the mind to

Activity 5. 3   10th Amendment Prop

Purpose: To help students understand the abstract concept of reserved powers in the United States Constitution through the use of a metaphor.

Using props brought into the classroom, demonstrate a sophisticated concept from social sciences in just moments. For this demonstration, you will need to make a large ball of papier-mâché, perhaps painting it with tempera to give the appearance of a large boulder. Also necessary will be a large colander with sizeable drain openings, a spaghetti strainer, a small tea strainer, and a hammer or rubber mallet. Drawing and using props throughout the demonstration will help students with the concept: an overhead projector, white board, chart with markers, or chalk board will suffice for the drawings as the explanation progresses.

recall the gist of the events, which serves as a framework for remembering exact details. Combining the narrative (sequenced story) with a visual (battlefield maps, photos, or drawings) helps students learn in chunks via intertwined memory networks. Creation of rich, stand-alone chunks that in some way "stick together" for the brain to comprehend is a way to help children remember information. Although helpful for organizing information, it is only one of several tools used to build student understanding.

ALTERNATIVE REPRESENTATIONS

New concepts must be communicated and demonstrated clearly as well, both by the teacher to students via instruction and then through student performance to prove understanding and mastery to the teacher. Learning does not automatically occur because facts are laid out in front of students: Successful teachers provide learning environments that *enable students to build meaning*.

Traditional methods of teaching rely heavily on verbal or written communication—in both teacher explanations and students responses—regardless of the subject area being taught. Children are asked to write explanations for a math solution in a journal and to define math-related terms. We expect the art student to write an essay answer to a test question on the role of color and texture in a work of art. Of course, if a lesson's goals *center on* improvement of language skills, then language manipulation is paramount in both the learning and assessment tasks. (Students must write to prove they have mastered writing skills!)

Figure 5.6 Visual Chunking

A Metaphor - 10th Amendment to the U. S. Constitution: Reserve Powers

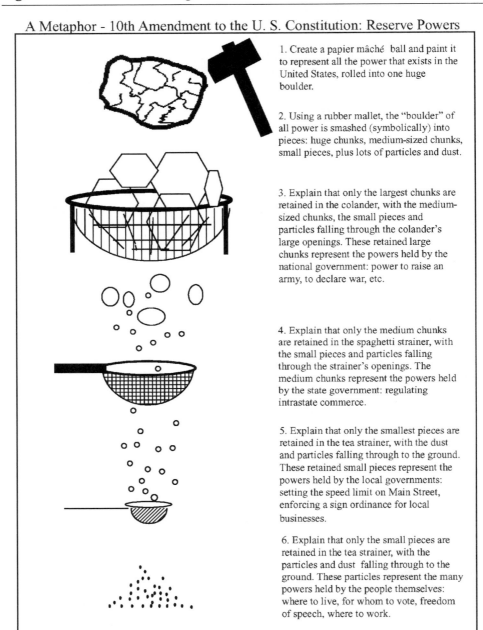

1. Create a papier mâché ball and paint it to represent all the power that exists in the United States, rolled into one huge boulder.

2. Using a rubber mallet, the "boulder" of all power is smashed (symbolically) into pieces: huge chunks, medium-sized chunks, small pieces, plus lots of particles and dust.

3. Explain that only the largest chunks are retained in the colander, with the medium-sized chunks, the small pieces and particles falling through the colander's large openings. These retained large chunks represent the powers held by the national government: power to raise an army, to declare war, etc.

4. Explain that only the medium chunks are retained in the spaghetti strainer, with the small pieces and particles falling through the strainer's openings. The medium chunks represent the powers held by the state government: regulating intrastate commerce.

5. Explain that only the smallest pieces are retained in the tea strainer, with the dust and particles falling through to the ground. These retained small pieces represent the powers held by the local governments: setting the speed limit on Main Street, enforcing a sign ordinance for local businesses.

6. Explain that only the small pieces are retained in the tea strainer, with the particles and dust falling through to the ground. These particles represent the many powers held by the people themselves: where to live, for whom to vote, freedom of speech, where to work.

If instructional goals are *not* language centered, however, students should be allowed demonstration of mastery through *nonlinguistic* representations (Marzano, Pickering, & Pollock, 2001). Such a reliance on language often causes language-challenged children unnecessary struggle. Success is easier to achieve when modalities appropriate for each child are honored, when mastery can be proven in ways independent of language. Both instruction

(Activity 5.4) and assessment tools can afford alternative ways of expressing meaning or demonstrating understanding. Activities 5.5 through 5.8 demonstrate additional possibilities for alternative expressions of meaning.

 Activity 5.4   Picture This

Purpose: To help improve comprehension and decoding of written text using kinesthetic activity.

Instruct students to listen carefully to a teacher-read story, as no illustrations will be shown to them. Explain to them that they will be asked to draw their *own* illustrations to reflect what they see within their mind as the words of the story are told. They will draw in sequence the events as they unfold, much like a comic book with no words. Model for the children an example of the process, using a brief story with which they are all familiar.

Next, provide each child with a clean sheet of paper and a crayon, pen, or marker. This visual journal is done with a permanent writing instrument, so the child does not become focused on erasing and refining artwork, but rather on creating a visual record of the story line. Begin reading slowly and with great expressiveness.

As soon as the story is complete, have children look at their visual record with a partner, comparing what they heard and revisiting the sequence of the story and the imagery that they saw.

Such an activity helps children develop their imaginations, enjoy imagery that they can personalize, understand the sequence of a story, and improve overall comprehension. Note: fairy tales, short and full of colorful language, are good material to use to introduce this process to children.

 Activity 5.5   Stellar Salad

Purpose: To use a visual representation, rather than verbal explanation, to help students understand the vastness of the solar system.

Prepare ahead to identify local landmarks well known to children that are proper distances from the school for purposes of illustrating this lesson. Bring to the classroom an array of common items for children to view, touch, or discuss as the lesson begins: a pumpkin (about 1 foot in diameter) or basket/red playground ball; a tomato, cut open to reveal seeds; a pea; a plum; a strawberry; a raisin; an

(Continued)

Activity 5.5 (continued)

apple; and a peach. After a brief discussion of relative sizes of items, comment that differences in size and the vastness of distance can be quite astounding and add that, in fact, today you are going to consider the size and scale of our *solar system*. Inform students that the pumpkin they are viewing is going to represent the sun, and you are going to take them on a virtual trip across our solar system. If possible, do much of this activity outside on school grounds.

Starting where the "sun" is placed, have students pace off 50 feet and gather around to view the tomato seed. Inform them that the seed represents the size of the planet Mercury, and its distance from the pumpkin represents the relative distance from the sun. Continue with the process as shown in Figure 5.7.

Figure 5.7

Stellar Salad

If the sun was a pumpkin about a foot in diameter . . .

• Mercury would be a tomato seed about 50 feet away

• Venus would be a pea about 75 feet away

• Earth would be a pea about 100 feet away

• Mars would be a small raisin, about 175 feet away

• Jupiter would be an apple about 550 feet away
(At the home run fence behind the ball diamond in the
  school yard)

• Saturn would be a peach about 1025 feet away
(Where the buses turn in to the school)

• Uranus would be a plum about 2050 feet away
(The corner of Palm Drive and Cordova Street)

• Neptune would be a plum about 3225 feet away
(Where the new gas station is near the library)

• Pluto would be smaller than a strawberry seed, nearly a
  mile away! (Where the freeway entrance is off Center Street)

Reprinted with permission: © Marilyn vos Savant and Parade Magazine, 2000.

Students will be astounded by the enormity of the solar system and not soon forget the impression! This activity not only uses alternative representations of a concept, it affords movement for the kinesthetic learner. It connects abstract ideas to the real world of a child (lesson based on material from the *Parade Magazine* "Ask Marilyn" column, April 30, 2000).

 Activity 5.6   Paint'n Tell

Purpose: To provide an artistic avenue for expression of understanding and communication of concepts.

After completing initial instruction on clouds through the use of pictures, observation, text, and direct instruction, have students express the shape and characteristics of nimbus, cirrus, cumulus, and stratus clouds in watercolor paintings. This can become an interdisciplinary exercise, with techniques in art aiding students in communication of science concepts.

 Activity 5.7   Movin' Math Grab Bag

Purpose: To help students construct meaning or express understanding in math using alternative representations of concepts.

Symmetry

To help students demonstrate *line symmetry*, use colorful pipe cleaners to create a visual example for children. Next, provide pipe cleaners of various colors to students, with directions that they produce their own example of line symmetry. The concept of line symmetry can be reinforced in a social studies, science, art, or literature unit through the making of papier-mâché masks. Once the concept of line symmetry is understood, ask students to create their own masks to represent a famous historical figure or a character in literature. The masks might be used as "talking heads," behind which children can stand to take on a character role or share facts about a celebrity.

Radial symmetry can be explained to and then demonstrated by students using square sheets of plain paper. Have students fold the paper in fourths and put an "X" in the center point as a starting and

(Continued)

Activity 5.7 (continued)

reference spot. Place any combination of lines, shapes, or symbols in each quadrant, located in the same position within each quadrant in relation to the center point X. After students create their own examples of radial symmetry, ask them to find examples in their world, such as pinwheels, sunrays, kaleidoscopes, flowers, and so on.

Multiplication of Fractions

To help students grasp *multiplication of fractions*, deal with it conceptually through manipulation rather than procedurally through a sequence of memorized steps. Explain to students that they are about to discover how to solve a problem such as 1/4 of 1/3 =? Instruct them directly that "of" means the same thing as times (×). Provide a full sheet of paper for each child, and then model for them the process shown in Figure 5.8.

Figure 5.8

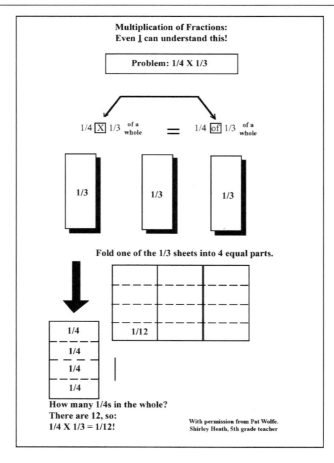

Instructing students to fold their sheet first into thirds, then one of the thirds into four parts, and then all thirds into four parts demonstrates clearly that, in fact, 1 of 4 parts of a third of a whole is really 1 of 12 parts of the whole. Concepts!

Fractions and Their Relative Sizes Can Be Explored

Sheets of paper can be used to represent a whole divided into parts. Use one sheet with two equal parts to demonstrate 2/2, one sheet with four parts to demonstrate 4/4, one sheet with eight parts to demonstrate 8/8, and so on. Provide each pair of students with one sheet of each configuration, and ask them to decide which is larger, 1/4 or 1/8, and why? Or to determine that if we ate 3/4 of a cake, would there be more or less than 1/6 of it left?

Ask students to pair up. To have students demonstrate knowledge of fractions without language, ask each child to use a square or rectangle of paper to demonstrate a fraction (1/3, 2/5, etc.) to his or her partner—using no words! Students might cut the paper, fold it, draw on it, or combine it with other papers to complete the task.

Math Terms

To rehearse and express the meaning of math terms, have students use their bodies (either standing or sitting) or popsicle sticks to demonstrate math concepts. For instance, the teacher might ask students to use the sticks to demonstrate vertex (or radius, angle, edge, face, and right angle) or use their bodies to show a neighbor what is meant by an acute angle and then change it to an obtuse angle (or perhaps circumference, radius). Have students create something that demonstrates the concept of parallel. Not only does body math afford choice in expression, it is an alternative way of communicating understanding—and an energizer! This task is great for the kinesthetic learner; it also allows for peer feedback.

 Activity 5.8   No Talk and All Action

Purpose: To help children feel rhythm, plus perceive variations in pitch in speech.

The brain must be exposed to the sounds, rhythms, and pitches of language to be ready for reading and spelling. It is changes in pitch

(Continued)

Activity 5.8 (continued)

that help brains understand spoken words, learn sounds for phonemes in language, and reconcile graphemes and phonemes for spelling.

To help pre-K and primary students improve pitch perception, use a slide whistle as a part of a daytime routine (perhaps to gain student attention at the end of an activity). When the students hear the distinct sound of the whistle, they will know to parrot back exactly the sound and pitches. This is a good exercise in listening, as well as in pitch and rhythm production.

To improve the detection and production of specific phonemes to help students gain experience in word differentiation, have students listen as they are given two different but similar-sounding words—such as *slush* and *flush*, *set* and *said*, or *moon* and *noon*—and ask them to replicate the sounds. This exercise can also be a transition ritual for learning activities; children must complete the sound echo before lining up to go to recess.

Make available small, dessert-sized paper plates for children to hold and use as they mirror vocal inflections, changes in pitch, or the rhythm of speech when the teacher tells a story or children listen to music. Let the paper plates become soft, tapping instruments that reflect the rhythm of the music; have the students move the plates increasingly higher as pitch or inflection rises and lower them when the voice drops (adapted from of Brewer & Campbell, 1991).

For older children learning and practicing proper punctuation (e.g., the use of commas, periods, and exclamation points), have students walk as they read a written passage of text. They stop in their tracks when they come to a period, they pause slightly with a comma, and they clap with an exclamation point. Making such kinesthetic moves while processing written punctuation will facilitate the proper use of such marks in their own writing. Improvement in the mechanics of writing is more likely!

This chapter began with a discussion of patterns, connections, and declarative memory, the accumulation of which provides the broad brushstrokes for a child's picture of the world. Initial experiences, like the baby with the puppy (see Chapter 1), establish a template for understanding four-legged animals. Yet the child experiences the category expanding and splitting exponentially upon seeing giraffes at the zoo, pigs at a fairground, horses in the picture film, and a photo of a lemur in a high school biology text. Subsequent experiences will help them detect defining features of categories, stored in memory, in new animals: four legs, fur, muzzles or elongated noses, and perhaps tails. But differences will be spotted as well, with new memory networks forming subcategories and subclassifications. A dog is small in size, a horse is large; each creature has its own distinct odor, its own color patterns. Children make sense of their world as they experience tasks, but we can help them see patterns and make solid connections through sound instructional delivery.

The work of many creative educators and sound thinkers provides us with tools to help children organize (Hyerle, 1996, 2000; and Warlick, 1998, 2001), chunk and categorize (Sousa, 2001 and Buzan, 1996), and construct meaning (Sylwester, 1995, 2000; Bruer, 1999; Stigler, 1999; Ratey, 2001; Costa and Bena Kallick, 2000, to name a few). Best practice includes skillful use of metaphors, analogies, and alternative representations in learning endeavors. It involves not just telling but also helping students construct their own meaning by planting connectable, retrievable, and adaptable memories.

6

Get Real!

Transferring Learning to Real Life

*Nothing ever becomes real till it is experienced—Even a proverb
is no proverb to you till your Life has illustrated it.*

—John Keats, 1795–1821

LEARNING FOR LIFE:
APPLICATION AND ADAPTATION

Learning results from the interaction of brain and body processed with a
backdrop of external and internal conditions, a sort of *dynamic intelligence*
(Sylwester, 2000). An experience, and hence memory, is more than the
sum total of sights, sounds, taste, smell, or the feel of the world. If it
was, we would all play the same music, dread the same activities, love
the same colors, and enjoy the same vegetables. There would be no need
for different political parties and little need for different points of view.
All humans would need is *reality*, and they would arrive at the same
conclusions!

Learning is not just amassing a huge body of trivial information but
acquiring knowledge and skills that can be transferred to *real-life* situations. Students must capable of applying concepts beyond the classroom,
beyond the context of summative (final) assessment. We have all known

the student who aces the test but has no clue how to apply the same content to real life. Educators must make clear the real-life emotional use of the information or skills, so students ". . . associate content with its usefulness" rather than with a test (Sylwester, 2000). Real-life learning activities that apply concepts in a practical fashion establish behavior templates, which can potentially empower the learner with strategies for life.

On the other hand, the underlying premise that characterizes drill and rote memorization is that external forces mold the mind: that a human mind stockpiles information and later makes appropriate connections to enable application of content or skills. The truth is that humans learn more efficiently through authentic, real-life tasks *within* instruction to build memory networks of *behavior* and *action*; that is, if they are truly transfering learning to the context of their lives.

For years, it was believed that meaning was constructed by assembling bits of inputted information into a whole, much like puzzle pieces fit together. The brain is likely more adaptive than that when processing information to construct meaning. Cognition (knowing) is closely related to action (I hear a car at an intersection so I pause and look both ways, or I hear a stirring speech and shed a tear). For learning to have meaning, it requires the interaction of current sensory input with neuronal networks (sensorimotor memories) that exist from earlier and somewhat similar experiences.

Behavior (response or output) can be reflexive (highly emotional, automatically processed, and often a primitive reaction to some stimulus: A horn beeps, and I jump) or reflective (requiring awareness and cognitive processing of a detail of a situation: leafing through a book to determine reading difficulty before checking it out of the library). Yet behavior may not be a simple, straightforward product where sensory information → reconstruction of meaning → reflex or reaction.

With reflective behavior, the brain's choice for action may depend not on whether environmental detail is correct but whether the contemplated behavior actually worked in the past! I washed windows with plain water, but they did not sparkle as they did when I put vinegar in the mix; so when polishing the glass table, I go for the vinegar bottle. The memory of these successes or failures of behavior/action become pointers, or patterns, of sensorimotor activity that ". . . categorize the world by behavior patterns." So behavior choices (action) are not so much a reaction to environmental stimulation, but are made based on expectations about a current situation that are rooted in previous experience and stored as memory (Engel, Fries, & Singer, 2001).

Learning for life, then, comes when tasks require children to form and experience strategies in problem solving. The result provides a rich cache of behaviors from which to choose—and deepens understanding of concepts! (See Activity 6.1.)

Figure 6.1

Reflective Behavior

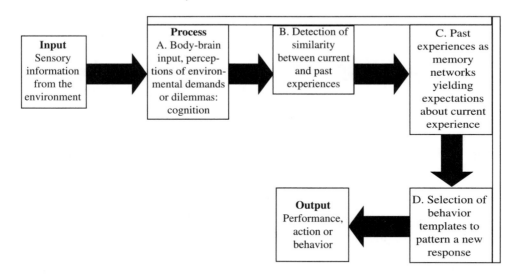

✳ **Activity 6.1**   Cookie Cutter

Purpose: To give children an opportunity to develop creative approaches for problem solving and then compare the effectiveness of all resulting strategies and applications.

Rather than introducing the concept of division and fractional parts through traditional instruction (modeling a procedure, practicing, and applying), ask students to solve the following dilemma in any fashion they want:

A friend invites over three classmates on a Saturday afternoon. He wants to offer his friends a snack of cookies, but discovers that there are only three left in the cookie jar. Four kids but only three cookies; how can the cookies be divided up evenly? Draw how you would do it.

Students might work in pairs, triads, or alone. They can arrange, talk, write, or use a computer or any method they want to solve the problem. After students arrive at solutions, they should be discussed in a whole-class debrief to measure each strategy's merits, shortcomings, and application. All children are exposed to an array of strategies as the teacher leads a discussion as to the relative practicality of each in solving the problem. Note that the task target (splitting evenly) is clear to children—and that it is real life.

How we acquire sensory input, process it, and respond to it is a result of many factors, including the interaction of emotion and multiple memory networks. Each time the human brain goes beyond its standard, existing memory network connections to process or respond, it literally grows *new* physical connections (synapses) between brain nerve cells. As new connections and new patterns are detected, one's personal picture of the world becomes clearer.

No child should be taught solely for successful performance on a test. Schools should prepare children for life, not for chapter tests. Therefore, sound learning goes beyond memorizing for the moment; the primary *reason* for studying must not be to pass a test, earn a grade, or please the teacher. To do that downplays the need to ever revisit the concept again. Students, instead, must be capable of adapting the new learning to the dilemmas of life—over and over again.

Reality is defined as "real things, or events as a whole," according to the *Random House Webster's School and Office Dictionary* (p. 377). It is neither mental calisthenics nor exercise done in isolation. Reality in the realm of learning is action in a context. It is not parroting information, but using skill or content to meet a human need in conjunction with the moment. It is demand tempered with condition and limitations. Real life *is* messy, not neat: It is steeped with trivial detail as well as that which is germane to a situation at hand. It includes choice as well as limitations, priorities as well as the extraneous. As Lewis Carroll wrote: "His answer trickled through my head, Like water through a sieve" (1872, p. 8).

Effective learning tasks, therefore, must also provide such limitation and distraction. To expect a child to automatically connect ideas or skills to the real world is unrealistic, as the average 13-year-old is not eager to employ formulas for surface area. Instruction must bridge that gap to help students see the usefulness of the facts, so the student who passes the math test with flying colors isn't dumbfounded when he or she is asked to create a 25-square-foot stage set in language arts class.

Mastery is proven in ways other than parroting information or repeating a skill component: Those are the *means* to an end. Breezing through objective and single-answer assessments or listing the steps in a scientific method sidesteps real-life contexts for content. Real mastery is proven in solutions reached from sorting and reflecting, predicting or estimating, hypothesizing, or evaluating results: *analytical skills*. It comes from combining information and skills in new ways: *creative skills*. It comes from finding real-life applications: *practical skills*. Skills (Sternberg, 1996)!

Notice the word *creativity* popping up. Not old templates, but *new* combinations. Learning how to dribble a basketball in physical education helps a player move the ball down court, but finding combinations of body moves to circumvent a defending player will score the points. Dividing six by eight is teachable, but the real value of learning comes when a child is given six candy bars and can find a way to split them evenly between eight cousins. New applications; improvisation!

WHAT'S IN IT FOR ME?

Brains are engaged when there is something captivating in an experience. Whether positive, negative, threatening or pleasurable, there is *something* in the experience to which the brain is drawn; something which touches human emotion or needs, inspiring attention to be paid. Even in learning environments where experiences are controlled (like a classroom), each student's brain sorts incoming stimuli to attend to that which is important at that moment in time. No student should ask, "Why do I have to learn this stuff? I'll never use it." One might say it is the brain's litmus test: "What's in it for me?" (WIIFM). Materials and learning activities need to have connections outside the artificial world of the classroom to help students find real-life examples of the concept (see Activity 6.2).

✳ **Activity 6.2   Sensory Imagery Skits**
_____

Purpose: To help readers better understand sensory imagery in prose and begin to infuse it into their own writing.

To introduce a lesson on visual imagery, the teacher acts out a scene, using only facial expressions and body movement, but no words. Students are asked to serve as detectives, noting as much detail as possible to describe subtleties of movement and change in the teacher's face and body. They should use scrap paper to jot down what they observe. Only observations are accepted, no assumptions: for example, " . . . raised eyebrow, hands over the head, crouched body, squinted eyes, open mouth," not "You looked scared." The teacher performs the scene at least two times, with exaggerated movement and expressions void of sound, in easy view of all students (perhaps expressing joy or pleasure by feigning the licking of an ice cream cone or acting out fear, disdain, confusion, or surprise). Next, students should share their observations, while the teacher records all responses. Redirect any assumptions ("You were afraid . . . "); instead, have students restate their ideas by describing what the body and face *did* ("You wrinkled your brow and drew back your head"). After the entire list is recorded, students should review all observations and determine what they communicate: *Now* a label can be applied to the scene. "You were terrorized!"

Place students into groups of three or four.[1] Each group member receives an envelope with a card containing an emotion that they will be asked to act out for their group. The remainder of the group will note the body and facial expressions of their classmates and then guess the emotion and details that they imply.

Help students define sensory imagery and explain how it draws pictures in a reader's mind. What they have done in acting, writers do with words: They provide clues and communicate meaning without labels.

Next, distribute short paragraphs (film clips or photos can also be used) filled with imagery, and ask students to read and infer what is happening and what characters are feeling:

> Paula stood far from the other girls as they jumped rope on the asphalt playground. Each took her turn; but as Paula neared them, the tallest girl tucked the rope under her arm and the entire group quickly walked back into the school building. Paula stood staring at the group as they disappeared, her head hung limply against her chest, her shoulders sloped downward. She turned slowly away, hands dug into her pockets, and kicked a rock across the dirt.

A follow-up might be to have each student choose some emotion (joy, sadness, exhaustion, fear, anger, frustration, or disgust) and write a paragraph using sensory imagery to communicate meaning clearly to the reader—without using the label itself. They create their own sensory imagery!

Real-life occurrences of skills and information can be spontaneous as well as planned. I recently observed a third-grade teacher instructing children in identification of word patterns for structural analysis in reading. It was a well-orchestrated, teacher-directed lesson that progressed as expected. Children responded with answers that satisfied the questions asked. But at the end of the lesson, the teacher improvised by asking students to extend learning with creative examples from their own minds and experience. The students came alive! Hands waved, and bodies that were previously slouched at desks lurched forward eagerly as children contributed their thoughts.

When debriefing the session later, I asked the teacher, "Which part of the lesson created energy and seemed most successful to *you*?" She thought for a moment and then apologetically said that it appeared the end of the lesson was the best. After pondering, she realized it was where students were challenged to create their own meaning through manipulation of a concept through discovery of patterns. Students were not just repeating back information but finding new applications in *their lives* for content and skills!

AUTHENTICITY IN TASKS

There is yet one more benefit for authentic tasks. The less text-based and the more life-based learning activities are, the easier concepts are recalled when needed by the learner. Common sense tells us that children learn fire drill procedures best by *experiencing* a drill. They hear the klaxon, close windows, turn out lights, line up against a specified wall, exit down a particular hallway, and line up silently in rows in the parking lot while their classroom teacher calls roll. If ever a fire occurred and students had to act, the environmental situation in the emergency would very closely resemble that of the learning context, making accurate retrieval of the memory more likely. You wouldn't expect students to understand emergency procedures simply by showing a video about fire drill procedures any more than by having them learn it by reading a text. And one cannot teach writing effectively if students only apply writing skills in a workbook. Activity 6.3 demonstrates one effective technique for improving imagery in writing.

 Activity 6.3   Long-Distance Learning Links

Purpose: To use reading and technology as a basis for authentic writing projects. Teacher preparations for this unit of study include visiting a Web site such as Web66 International Schools Registry (A listing of all schools in the world: http://web66.coled.umn.edu/schools.html) or Global SchoolNet (a site for announcing or looking for collaborative projects: http://www.gsn.org/pr/).

Locate and contact a school in the geographic location where an upcoming piece of literature is set. Ideally, the story's setting should be in a region very different than that in which the children live to allow for unique experiences for all children involved. Contact a teacher of the same grade level in the chosen school and enlist his or her cooperation in a collaborative reading effort to be undertaken by the two classrooms. The task will involve both classes of children, one in the story location and one elsewhere, who read the story simultaneously, using student e-mail to (a) compare reactions and feelings about the story, (b) ask questions about the respective geographic regions, and (c) establish lines of ongoing communication between students. A teacher from South Carolina might choose a story such as *Julie of the Wolves* by Jean Craighead George, set in the North Slope of Alaska. Explain to the children that the way they will read their next story will be different, as they will have reading "partners" from Alaska. Students will be paired with counterparts in the collaborating school, perhaps from Nunivak Island, where the main character was born, or the city of Barrow. They will write on a daily basis to share and compare feelings, reactions, and questions. The South Carolina students, for instance, might react with sadness at the death of a wolf, whereas the Alaskan children may treat the same event with as much concern as a South Carolina child would if a squirrel was hit on the roadway. This task is a great way to understand perspective, see new regions through others' eyes, learn about different geographic locations, and establish pen pals. Children will have reason for careful written communication and a sudden concern for clarity and accuracy in spelling and punctuation, and form will become real! Writing will have purpose, and literature will come alive.

It is through such emotion-based WIIFM activities that children realize the connection to " . . . the real-life emotional uses of the information" (Sylwester, 2000, p. 37). Following patterns established by Beane and Lipka (1986) in *Self-Concept, Self Esteem and the Curriculum*, teachers can make academic topics relevant to the world of the youngster.

GROWING INTELLIGENCE

In the past century, through work done Alfred Binet (Binet & Simon, 1916), intelligence was judged by performance on standardized, norm-referenced tests. They primarily measured skills of logic, mathematics, and language. But since the early 1970s, new ideas from the likes of Howard Gardner (1991, 1997), Robert Sternberg (1996), David Perkins (1992, 1995), William Calvin (1996), Daniel Goleman (1995), Joseph LeDoux (1996), Robert Sylwester (1995, 2000), Mihaly Csikszentmihalyi (1997), and Arthur R.

Figure 6.2

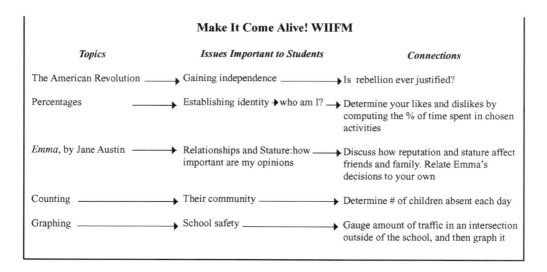

Jensen (1998) (to name a few) have flooded our profession and expanded our definition of intelligence.

Perhaps Jean Piaget was closest to correct, however, in saying that intelligence is what we use *when we don't know what to do*. As neurophysiologist William Calvin implies, intelligence is exhibited by a person whose life is rich in experiences and who possesses a huge pool or repertoire of retrievable memory experiences. When a new dilemma or problem is presented in that person's life, the brain is capable of reaching into the repertoire—not to find totally new thoughts but to pull together related experiences and ideas to recombine them to provide a solution; it discovers some underlying order. But, as David Perkins says in *Outsmarting IQ: The Emerging Science of Learnable Intelligence*, "Nothing counts like a rich fund of experience" (p. 82). It might be looking at a never-before-seen leaf and accurately being able to call it a type of maple based solely on a few traits common to all maples. But it could also be a kindergartner observing the movement of clock hands, watching the order cards are played in a game of hearts at the kitchen table at home, and then later "knowing" the correct direction to move the token around the game board in Parcheesi.

Finding meaning and application in one's life changes the purpose of knowledge from isolated trivia to a useful tool. Successfully choosing correct punctuation marks for a sentence in a multiple-choice quiz is one thing; using correct punctuation in one's own writing is another. A student might easily name the major disease-causing bacteria and explain their

Figure 6.3

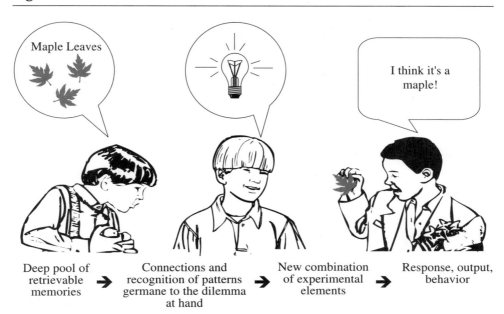

Deep pool of retrievable memories → Connections and recognition of patterns germane to the dilemma at hand → New combination of experimental elements → Response, output, behavior

characteristics to ace the health class test. But ask this same student to safeguard his or her own family against disease while on a vacation camping trip, and he or she may have no idea what steps to take. Classroom learning scenarios need to engage the human brain and motivate students to learn *because there is a reason to do so*. "What's in it for me?" will be a question of the past in your classroom.

The focus of this chapter is on academic learning for life through making connections, borrowing from behavior templates, discovering new combinations, and taking some informed action. Mastery is key but so, too, is retrieval of the new skill or concept. Research at both Harvard Medical School in Boston and Hadassah University Hospital in Israel has found that although learning new skills and content requires great activation of the cerebral cortex, once the skill is *mastered* its reactivation becomes more automatic. Its entrenched presence in long-term memory changes the processing center from the cerebral cortex to the cerebellum and midbrain region (more primitive parts of the brain) to free up the cerebral cortex for dealing with newer content or skills (Ratey, 2001).

Practice and rehearsal of new learning does matter, because they make possible the transition to automaticity (retrievable, usable memory in the pool of memories) and allows the cerebral cortex to spend increased activity on new skills. The pool of automatic, easily retrieved, engrained memory deepens. Experience counts. Practice counts more, because the more one can do, the more one can do.

The twenty-first century is a *thinking* century. Career projects and adult tasks are often so complex that they require the collaboration of *many* skilled people to reach creative solutions. Thus, individual mastery and replication of a static body of information is no longer adequate for maneuvering in the world of work. Tomorrow's adults will need to *apply* an ever-expanding body of information in new, unique scenarios to strategize and discover solutions to arising dilemmas. Skill is taken to a new level: one of problem solving, creating, and applying. Dynamic intelligence.

NOTE

1   Research tells us that group size does matter. Marzano, Pickering, and Pollock (2001) report in *Classroom Instruction That Works* that small groups composed of three to four members appear more effective than larger groups. Pairing students improves performance over no grouping, but groups of three to four show the largest percentile gain. Larger groups or five to seven students, however, actually experience a small *decline* in performance (Lou, Abrami, Spence, Paulsen, Chambers, & d'Apollonio, 1996).

7

Who Said
It Couldn't Be Done?

Blueprints for Student Success

If a thing is humanly possible, consider it to be within your reach.

—Marcus Aureluis Antoninus, 121–180

Take calculated risks. That is quite different from being rash.

—George Smith Patton, 1885–1945

CHALLENGE

To keep the brain honed for survival, challenge is necessary to activate the brain with opportunities to innovate. Within a nurturing, sensibly protective environment, it enables the child to adjust and grow.

Challenge implies the presence of a demand, perhaps even a contest. In the midst of *academic* challenge, there is a call to go beyond standard solutions in order to meet some demand. If a child is asked to locate information on lowland gorillas, his or her search may not end in a textbook, which contains only three sentences about the animal. He or she may search library books, videos, and Internet sources before contacting the curator at the city's zoo to gather the best facts possible. But through the search, a student gains an ever-expanding understanding of how to operate within her world. Different experiences in related contexts enable a learner to spot common characteristics and thus problem solve within the safety of a familiar framework. Enough experiences in grocery stores, for instance, enables one to maneuver in any grocery store anywhere in the country—not because they are identical, but because the brain hooks into memory networks that help it spot patterns common to many. These serve as templates—or blueprints—for comparing new experiences to old. As one spots patterns, he or she manages behavior with increasing confidence and becomes ever more worldly (and able to find the mayonnaise within two minutes in a 15,000-square-foot store). Finding mayonnaise can be accomplished via a direct trek down the condiment aisle, by circling through the meat department, or by methodically weaving through each row in the store. There are many ways to locate mayonnaise (an open-ended task invites multiple solutions!).

Within a classroom, however, there are times when only one acceptable answer exists. After all, 7 times 7 is always 49 and a teacher would be remiss to accept an incorrect, albeit creative, answer from his or her students. There are times, of course, when rote memory is both efficient and necessary. Yet when only one answer is acceptable, a student will likely labor only until the answer that satisfies the task is found. Rewards come for parroting content, not for going beyond it or synthesizing new concepts with it. A call for the repetition of knowledge or the replication of a skill is low-level thinking on Bloom's Taxonomy, Cognitive Domain (Bloom, 1956).

Classrooms that challenge provide learning experiences that invite unique combinations of content and creative combinations of skills to solve problems. Children go beyond memorizing content to *using* content. Teachers who provide learning tasks that nudge the child beyond comprehension and straight application foster skill development in their students. Tasks (such as in Activity 7.1) that require repetitive use of the skill encourage mastery.

 Activity 7.1   Flagpole

Purpose: To help students make the connection between math concepts and real life through challenging, authentic tasks.

Present a practical dilemma for students to solve in a plane geometry class:

The school board has asked the principal at a neighboring grade school to price a three-foot-wide flagstone path to the flag pole in front of the school, as the foot traffic to the pole has killed the grass. The board has only five hundred dollars to invest in the project, and since flagstone costs three dollars per square foot installed, they need to get an estimate of cost before the project goes forward. The maintenance crew is stretched thin with work, so the principal has asked the eighth-grade math class at the district middle school to make the calculations.

Give students the following diagram, which contains the only information available from the grounds crew, and ask them to make a recommendation to the principal regarding the construction of the walkway from point C to point A. Students should work in small groups to solve the problem, followed by a whole-class debrief of possible strategies. This helps students combine an authentic task with challenge, the entire time manipulating math concepts; involving practice, practice, practice; and contributing to the deepening of memory.

Figure 7.1 Practical Application for Geometry

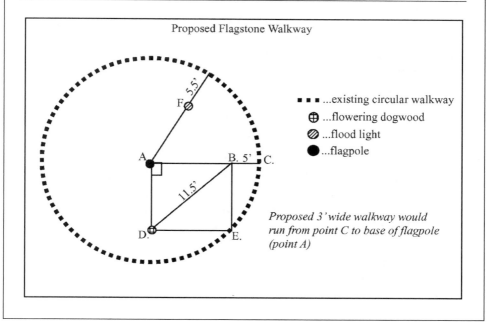

As student skills improve, neurotransmitters (brain chemicals that carry neural instructions within the brain) can be affected. One such neurotransmitter is serotonin, which affects brain function and attitude. As Robert Sylwester pointed out in a speech at the 1996 ASCD National

Convention, optimum serotonin levels mean higher self-esteem, more self-assuredness, and more mellow and assertive behavior (2000, p. 125). As humans succeed and gain confidence, serotonin levels increase. Success, then, perhaps does breed success.

STRESS VERSUS RISK

A common concern in challenging children, however, is that it can cause stress. Excessive stress is counterproductive to learning, not to mention to the emotional health of the child (Caine & Caine, 1997a). It appears that the human response to perceived threats, when accompanied by feelings of "... helplessness or fatigue ..." can bring on a lack of self confidence, reducing our ability to "... engage in complex intellectual tasks, those requiring creativity and the ability to engage in open-ended thinking and questioning" (Caine & Caine, 1997a, p. 103, referencing Caine, Caine, & Crowell, 1994, p. 70). Yet stress is *not* synonymous with risk: Because the former is imposed from the outside, the latter is *self-chosen*. A challenge for one child may be an unreasonable demand for another and yet a "snap" for a third. When rigidly paced, lock-step expectations are set for proving mastery—regardless of the range of developmental and ability levels within any classroom—stress will result for *somebody*. To avoid it, multiple solutions reflective of an equally broad range of possibilities for meeting criteria should be encouraged. By their very nature, such open-ended tasks invite improvisation commensurate to one's abilities and allow creativity while demanding higher level thinking from all (see Activity 7.2).

 Activity 7.2   It's Music to My Ears

Purpose: To cause the application of content knowledge in music in a challenging way, where students produce (synthesize) a musical product according to rigid parameters in a learning task, yet with limitless levels of sophistication possible to reflect the ability level of each child.

Upon completion of direct instruction relating to musical concepts, students are assigned a task with a musical product for homework. The following are the product requirements: (1) Produce a four-measure tune, (2) use at least one half note and two quarter notes in your tune, and (3) use 3/4 time. Students must revisit course content, problem solve to meet the criteria set for the task, and produce a product that expresses understanding of the concepts. One student may simply repeat a half note and quarter note combination for four

---

measures, and one may write an involved, sophisticated tune with rests and more! Each, however, would be able to successfully meet the criteria set, regardless of sophistication, as the parameters set for mastery were clear.

Curriculum standards should drive such open-ended tasks. Yet not every child reaches the target in the same fashion, at the same speed, or with the same facility. Lowering standards is not the answer to eliminating stress: Allowing students to prove mastery in a multitude of ways, through challenging tasks with multiple solutions, is. Low expectations often translate into low achievement. Children need practice in problem solving if they are to successfully meet challenges both in and out of school. Learning tasks must demand—and then reward—successful mastery and application of concepts.

OPEN-ENDED TASKS, MULTIPLE SOLUTIONS

Learning tasks that involve low-level thinking skills (knowledge, comprehension, and application) routinely reward predetermined responses from students. Generally, only one answer is acceptable. Academic challenge is characterized by increased complexity of content or larger quantities of material to master, not by innovative thinking or problem solving. Even with extremely complicated material, predefined combinations of concepts result in predictable conclusions.

Such a consistent call for replication and uniformity makes content/skill an *end* rather than a *means* to an end. Learning is static and defined. This type of "intelligence" is inert, because it does not synthesize, it does not create. How this approach sells learning short! According to Robert Sternberg, Professor of Psychology and Education at the College of Education at Yale University, " . . . intellectual abilities [are] dynamic and flexible rather than . . . static and fixed" (1996, pp. 32-33). Activity 7.3 encourages dynamic intelligence.

 Activity 7.3   Web Analysis

Purpose: To ask students to think creatively and critically to uncover complex and multiple effects that flow from single sources.

Using carefully worded prompts, pose a question that invites critical thinking, a sequenced chain of predictions about a hypothetical

(Continued)

Activity 7.3 (continued)

event: "What would happen if oil tankers were outlawed?" This task is concerned with possibilities and not with realities stemming from an event or idea. Next, introduce a series of interconnected, complex and multiple effects that flow from a single event or source: "What effect did September 11, 2001, have on the world? What were the effects of the Columbine High School shootings?" This task is concerned with realities and outcomes. Have students use visual organizers, such as webs, to show cause and effect, relationships, interconnectedness, and so on. Note: This activity is easily adaptable to different fundamental learning areas; for instance, prompts can be used that deal with themes or conflicts in literature, questions in science or social studies, and issues in health or the environment.

Figure 7.2   Web Analysis

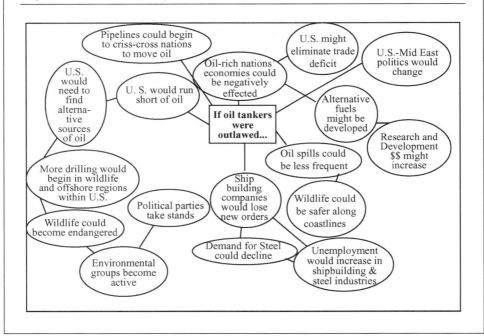

If information is learned devoid of a real-life context, the student might be capable of listing reasons why oil tankers would be outlawed by an act of Congress. But use critical thinking to explore consequences and evaluate actions? No guarantees there. Is it any wonder that extremely successful students in our schools often fall short in achieving success in life? It seems many are prepared—solely to take tests!

Higher level thinking differs from simple application in that it involves creative manipulation (analysis, synthesis, and evaluation, according to

Figure 7.3   Prepared . . . or Unprepared?

Bloom's Taxonomy, Cognitive Domain). Challenging tasks invite potentially unique products, with evaluations of the product (solution) based on criteria (targeted qualities of the project) to guide student work. At any point in the learning task, a student can compare his or her progress against markers of excellence, a kind of yardstick. Synthesis (product) and evaluation (judgment of the product in relationship to criteria) are at the highest level of Bloom's Taxonomy.

When children measure the distance between Columbus and Cleveland, Pittsburgh and Philadelphia, or Sacramento and Fresno using map scales to determine distance between cities, they perform with lower level skills. Higher level skill might demand the use of content or skills in the midst of a messy, real-life situation: "If you won a travel prize from a local radio station for four free trips to cities of your choice within a seven hundred fifty-mile radius of your hometown of Philadelphia, Pennsylvania, which four cities would you visit?" Such a scenario affords several approaches to correct solutions, but demands manipulation of course content.

For example, let's say you propose that the students decorate the classroom for an event. Choice abounds as children decide if they want decorations on all four walls or only on the front. And in fact, they must decide if there should be wall decorations at all: How about a mobile, or a piñata, or spending money on balloons instead of metallic fringe rope? In the process of solving the problem, they are challenged by an authentic and interdisciplinary task. There is a call to apply art elements of balance and color; there is a math application to determine the number of rolls of (let's say) crepe paper the room would require and if the plan fits the allotted budget. Students need to read labels on crepe paper rolls to see how many running feet each provides and use speaking and listening skills to inquire from the office about school safety rules. (See Activities 7.4 and 7.5.)

 Activity 7.4   Party Plan

Purpose: To help students improve math skills in a challenging, open-ended learning task that requires content manipulation as well as problem-solving skills.

Assign students, working in groups of two to four, the task of decorating for a birthday party. They can choose any decoration theme they would like, but must work within these guidelines:

- Only $19.75 is in the decorating fund
- Decorations can cover as much or as little of the classroom as they choose: the ceiling, the walls, the floor, or any parts thereof
- School rules prohibit using any materials that require permanent changes to the building or janitorial services to clean up
- Decorations must create an air of celebration
- All decorations must be put up and taken down by students, following school safety rules

---

 Activity 7.5   Rhythm Shuffle

Purpose: To help students learn note values through creative combinations to produce personal rhythms.

After instruction and assessment of understanding of note values (perhaps eighth notes, quarter notes, half notes, and whole notes) ask students to volunteer taking turns by arranging a rhythmic pattern of their choice to provide a measure of note combinations correct for 4/4 time (or 3/4 time, etc.). Students choose cards that represent note values to correctly add up to the beats for a given meter. As children contribute their combinations, the class will help determine the correctness of the combination. Then the entire class performs (with claps or percussion instruments) each unique rhythm.

There are as many possibilities, considerations, and combinations as there are children making the decisions. Each child might have a unique solution, and each can be as correct as every other. But in the process, the child is going to have to measure portions or elements of the room to solve the problem! Keep in mind the words of Lyndon Baines Johnson: "If two men agree on everything, you may be sure that one of them is doing the thinking" (Bartlett, 1983). To encourage creative approaches in writing, look to Activity 7.6.

✳ Activity 7.6   Story Spaghetti

Purpose: To involve children in an open-ended task requiring classifying and editing details from a story, using a graphic organizer to help children successfully write the body paragraphs of a five-paragraph basic expository writing form.

Begin by telling children a special story is going to be read to them as they read their own copy silently. Use a colorful, engaging story filled with descriptions of a main character and his or her actions or appearance. Ask each child to listen and think about what the character is like as the story unfolds. Children are then given time to reread the story themselves, this time noting observations about the character and recording their observations. Students then form small groups, first to share individual observations and then to scour the text and extract additional details about the main character to record as a group assignment. These must include only what is observed (not inferred) about the character, supported by passages from written text. In a full-class discussion, record all ideas in a round-robin fashion, perhaps ideas such as "She had a twisted, snarling face," "She went back on her word and did not give her her freedom even though she promised," or "She kicked the cat."

(Continued)

Activity 7.6 (continued)

Provide students limited practice in forming categories and identifying common features of members of a category (e.g., by combining apples, oranges, and bananas because they are all fruit or coins, balls, and drinking glasses because they all have round parts). Announce that ideas, like tangible things, can also be grouped based on a common trait. When asked if there are two observations from the story that seem to go together, children might couple "She had a snarling face" with "She had an evil grin." Code the original observations as they are sorted to designate the relationship to other related observations, perhaps with colored bullets or special symbols for members of each category. The process should continue until every observation from the original whole-class debrief list is sorted into a category.

Figure 7.4   Three Body Paragraph Organizer

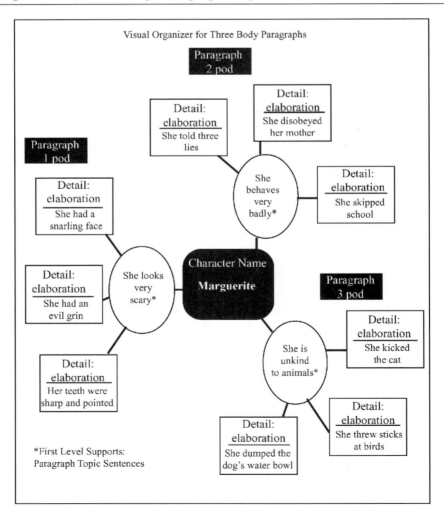

Next, have the class reach consensus on labels which identify the common feature for all the elements of each category (perhaps all have to do with appearance, behavior, actions, or feelings), making certain that the label holds true for each observation within the category. There may be three, four, or five categories. As long as the trait that children identify applies to all items in a given category, it is important that novel grouping patterns be accepted. It is the process and creativity of the children, not the teacher, that is being developed!

Once categories are formed and items are coded, each is cut out of the chart into a strip. They are physically grouped by color to later serve as details—elaboration—and second-level supports in the impending writing project. Next, introduce a visual organizer.

Have students return to their small groups and agree on at least three observations from one of the charted categories that seem to best go together for them. Have them plug those in to the detail circles of the visual organizer and then determine a statement which best describes what those details say about the main character (e.g., "She had a very scary face" or "She behaves very badly"). Each pod of the visual organizer becomes a representation of a single, fully developed body paragraph for an essay! Repeat the process for other major categories posted to complete the entire essay.

The visual organizer helps students make connections between observations and see patterns for organizing thoughts into a written product. Statements describing the category become first-level supports (topic sentences) for the essay's body paragraphs. Observation details become the second-level supports, or the elaboration. Note: Children can use their essays with an authentic audience. Invite children to write the essay to their parents or a student from another class to introduce them to characters in the story.

CREATIVITY IS NOT JUST IMAGINATION

Notice that creativity is not simply an exercise in imagination—it is imagination coupled with knowledge and tempered with judgment. Novel, unique solutions result from new combinations of neural networks within the brain, a result of some challenge that calls for a brain to go beyond standard, preexisting neural connections. According to William Calvin, a base of existing knowledge is required for any versatility. But creativity and intelligent behavior come not from new ideas, but ". . . new combinations of old things" (Calvin, 1996, p. 24). (See Activity 7.7.)

✳ **Activity 7.7**   Dying Plants

Purpose: To improve problem-solving skills in an open-ended task using a cooperative learning process.

Begin a multi-day learning task by focusing on a unit of study on the life cycle of green plants. Set up the learning scenario by informing students that all classroom plants died in the science room during last year's 2-week winter break. With a 16-day winter break looming, ask the students to come up with a solution to avoid the death of classroom plants over this year's long holiday.

- Lead a whole-class discussion to state the problem clearly
- Have students generate, either in small groups first and/or whole-class sharing, criteria that might be used to judge what solution is best. List as many student-generated criteria as possible, followed by a selection process to whittle the list to the three or four most important
- Have students work in teacher-assigned triads to identify several possible solutions for the problem. Each group explains their proposals before the entire class; lead a discussion to identify possible sources of information for each solution (see Figure 7.5)
- Assign a group task to explore two to three possible solutions, seek evidence, and arrive at a recommendation for saving the plants. The group will present its recommendation before the entire class

Small groups will reconvene over several class periods to (a) discuss and determine the suggested solutions (two to four) they will research and explore (each group selects from the class-generated list of proposals); (b) gather information needed to arrive at a conclusion through interviews, text searches, Internet sources, media center materials, and so on; (c) determine the advantages and disadvantages of each proposed solution; and (d) arrive at their group recommendation for the solution to the problem. Only criteria established by the entire class at the onset of the learning task guide their decisions and final proposal.

After group work is complete, each student signs off on the team proposal form (Figure 7.5). The team presents their proposal to the class, explaining and self-critiquing their chosen solution. Note: The self-evaluation piece allows the students to assess their successes and their shortfalls. Was the criteria list complete enough to allow optimum evaluation of solutions? Have they determined what the classroom plants need to remain healthy and alive? Had they ascertained what killed last year's plants? Did they ask enough questions, gather enough background information, research enough facts, and use the best resources? What would they change if they again approached a problem? What strategies would they recommend to others trying to solve dilemmas?

Figure 7.5   Organizing for Problem-Solving

Statement of the Problem:
What actions must we take to avoid having all the potted plants in the science room die over our 16-day winter vacation?

Criteria for judging a solution:
• It is affordable
• It is allowable
• The plants are alive when we return from vacation

Possible Solutions	Sources/Resources	Advantages	Disadvantages
A. Each student takes home a plant to care for	• Check with parents • Text book about how to care for plants xxxxxxxxxxxxxxx xxxxxxxxxxxxxxx	• Nobody gets stuck with lots of work xxxxxxxxxxx xxxxxxxxxxx xxxxxxxxxxx	• Lots of students will be out of town during vacation xxxxxxxxxxxxx xxxxxxxxxxxxx xxxxxxxxxxxxx
B. The custodians will water the plants every day	• Check with Custodians and Principal xxxxxxxxxxxxx xxxxxxxxxxxxx	• It is easy because plants do not have to be moved xxxxxxxxxxxx xxxxxxxxxxxx	• Our custodians don't know how to care for plants xxxxxxxxxxxxx xxxxxxxxxxxxx
C. Buy an automatic watering system	• Local garden store • Principal and teacher for permission to use cords and electricity xxxxxxxxxxxxx	• No one has to tend to the plants xxxxxxxxxxxx xxxxxxxxxxxx xxxxxxxxxxxx	• It is expensive • If there is a leak, it could cause a flood • Principal says no xxxxxxxxxxxxx

Recommendation:	Team debrief notes and self-evaluation:
	Team Signatures:

Figure 7.6 Lower vs. Higher Level Skills

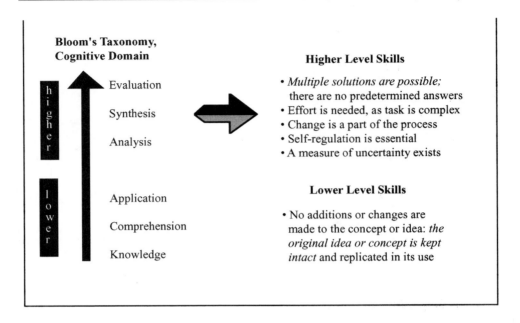

So creative, higher level thinking *requires* risk taking by students (often made easier and safer through group collaboration and consensus). Creativity transports students beyond the obvious to new, imaginative responses and products. The highest levels of thinking, including evaluation, should be driven by standards-related criteria within a classroom (see Chapter 4). Mastery of content is not the end itself as subject area content plays a key role as a *vehicle* in performance of the task: The process grows new connections within the brain's architecture and is where learning occurs, and the product is proof of learning progress!

SELF-ESTEEM AND CHALLENGE

> *A man of genius makes no mistakes. His errors are volitional and are the portals of discovery.*
>
> —James Joyce, 1882–1941

Educators are rightly concerned about building self-esteem in children. In recent past decades, the perception has been that guaranteed success improves self-esteem. The quest for safe learning environments, however, has often resulted in increasingly easier task requirements to ensure that more students *can* succeed. Yet no matter how simple a learning activity is, invariably it will require too little from some students and expect too much from others. So concern for the performance of lower ability students gave rise to lowered expectations for all. It was the only way, in a lockstep-recall method of learning, to avoid undue stress for struggling learners.

But avoiding failure for all students is impossible at best and undesirable at worst. It requires removal of any *likelihood* to err. Yet errors are inevitable when one steps beyond the bounds of certainty, when the untested, the untried, or the nonstandard approach is chosen. If educators punish error, students will choose safety and stick to the "tried and true," reactivating and retracing the old established memory networks. That is not learning, it is reviewing! Avoidance of failure brings avoidance of risk taking. It puts a limit on the expectations for learning, a sort of cognitive glass ceiling.

Educators who encourage measured academic risk taking help all students (high and low ability, special needs, and at risk) to attain higher learning levels. Errors transform into learning opportunities if children are made to correct and reflect upon them. Whereas success teaches it what to repeat, mistakes teach the brain what to avoid. *Intelligent people do not avoid mistakes; intelligent people avoid repeating them.* Self-esteem, that lofty goal for youngsters, is a by-product of meaningful experience. Nathaniel Branden, Ph.D., practicing psychologist at the Biocentric Institute of Los Angeles says, "Comfort is not self-esteem—it is not lowering standards until everyone can master them with little pain or effort" (Branden, 1987, p. 9). The surest path to high self-esteem might then be to *allow people to be successful at something* they *deem to be difficult*. That "thing" might be different for each person, but to eliminate a child's reasonable struggle, we rob him or her of the opportunity to build self-confidence. Opportunities must be provided for students to feel good about themselves through invitations to take risks, struggle through reasonable and developmentally appropriate challenges, and *build* self-esteem. Activity 7.8 provides both invitation to risk and challenge.

 Activity 7.8   Controversy Continuum

Purpose: To improve elaboration and support for opinions stated in persuasive writing. Focusing on a controversial issue, students will express and support opinions via simulations, debate, skits, and discussion.

Provide written material on some controversial issue pertinent to the subject being taught (e.g., for social studies, a particular amendment;

(Continued)

Activity 7.8 (continued)

for language arts, a story theme; or for science, an ethical issue). After reading the following article, students should take a stand either pro local merchants or pro street vendors.

> In the town of St. Augustine, Florida, a war of words has been waging for more than two years over the rights of vendors, street performers, and street artists to do business on the main street of this tourist town—and the rights of local merchants to pressure lawmakers to pass ordinances against them. Long hailed as the oldest city continuously occupied in North America, more than two million visitors trek the cobblestone walk that is the main artery through the historic district, St. George Street.
>
> At last week's city council meeting, hundreds of people representing both sides of the argument attended and spoke regarding the issue. The mayor, himself a local businessman and owner of the largest eating establishment in the historic district, voiced objections to the vendors and artists. "Patrons cannot see my signs nor easily move past the crowds watching performers. What used to be a lucrative walk-by business has become nonexistent." Echoing those concerns was the coalition of merchants on Cuna Street, the artery blocked daily by the performing "tin man." "The crowds routinely huddle around the performer," spokesperson Taylor Garcia says, "and prohibit any but the boldest tourists from pushing through and around the clogged roadway to enter our shopping area. My business has dropped from $3500 net income monthly to barely over $1700 since these charlatans have come. I will not be able to pay my rent soon."
>
> Kevin Moriarty, a musician whose livelihood depends upon public performances, claims that his rights to free speech are violated if he is run off St. George Street. "I am just a struggling businessman, who cannot afford the astronomical rents charged to set up permanent shop in St. Augustine. I have three children and a mortgage to support, and I am doing it in a moral, legal, and entrepreneurial way. It seems to me that the wealthier businessmen are attempting to drive the small businessman out of work—there is more than enough business for us all. No street vendor or performer has ever been found to purposely block a doorway or entrance to any established and permanent business in the city, and so it seems ruthless to penalize us for the problems of heavy foot traffic. Many visitors claim that one main attraction to the old city is the presence of street artists and vendors, adding color and excitement to a vacation spot. Without us, there would

probably be less income for even the regular housed businesses. We are an attraction, not a distraction or detriment! This is a question of discrimination against the poor, and an inordinate amount of consideration for the already wealthy!"

Using a long wall that accommodates the students in a single-file line, construct a continuum from 1 to 10. Have each student place himself or herself (article in hand) on a chosen point of this continuum, depending upon his or her degree of agreement with either extreme: 1 means full agreement with the merchants and 10 means full agreement with the street vendors.

Once students are positioned on the continuum, begin asking challenging questions, such as "Why do you side with the vendors?", "Merchants, why would a vendor feel this way?", "How would the tourists feel?", "Where did you get that information?", "What is the City Commission's stand?", and "Who has checked the financial records?" Force students to think critically, question, and probe truth. Perhaps ask them, after several minutes of debate, to argue the opposite point of view rather than their own.

Record any additional information or facts that must be sought to clarify positions as the exercise continues. Inform students that real critical thinking involves not just forming an opinion and arguing it, but being willing to change position when the evidence warrants it. (There should be some shift in position on the continuum when sound arguments are made.)

One or more class periods should now be spent in research, such as Internet searches, letter writing, text checking, and fact verification to answer questions and fill in missing information as recorded during the continuum discussion.

Pair students and assign each a role as either a vendor or a merchant to represent the respective points of view. Roles are assigned randomly and are not necessarily reflective of a student's point of view.

Project on the overhead the short, scripted position statements for the vendor and the merchant. Each statement will be chorale read by those students role playing the respective position. The following is a sample scenario:

Person A, the Merchant: Shoppers cannot get into my store

- **1st round**: I have to pay taxes to reap the benefits of public services—all should share the burden.
- **2nd round**: You have no right to shortcut to privilege. I had to borrow money and risk my income and security to lease a storefront. Why shouldn't you?

(Continued)

Activity 7.8 (continued)

Person B, the Vendor: I have the right to freedom of expression.

- **1st round**: All Americans have the right to public access. I do not benefit from the protection of buildings, air conditioning, and trash removal facilities, so why should I have to pay?
- **2nd round**: I cannot afford to pay rent and have overhead, but should I not have a right to work hard and make a life?

Next, project probing questions on the overhead for the pairs to discuss, for example:

- Question A: What is the responsibility of the individual businessperson to the community?
- Question B: What is the responsibility of the community toward individual businesses?
- Question C: What is the responsibility of individual businesspersons to other businesses in the immediate area?

Provide 3–5 minutes for pairs to respond to each, inviting students to argue from differing perspectives and to consider the complexity of the issue. They may spot inconsistencies in reasoning, discover that information is missing to reach sound conclusions, or spot general concerns that require further research. Assign group pairs to each write a two-student skit, 3–4 minutes in length, that would be indicative of expected dialogue between supporters of opposing points of view. Skits are performed and discussed in front of the whole class. It may be necessary to follow with another research session.

Final Activity: Have each individual student write a persuasive paper on the following topic: "Is it proper to pass local ordinances to limit the rights of street performers, vendors, and artists?" (The product could also be a debate, piece of art work, political cartoon, or a response to a piece of literature reflective of a similar question or theme.)

Comfort is key. Through modeling and reasonable expectations, children are encouraged to take risks and gain in confidence within a framework containing clear guidelines. Affording sufficient personal choice to prove mastery of a concept or skill, the abilities and preferences of each learner will be accommodated.

MOTIVATION

Students, if rarely challenged, can become comfortable in neat, tidy learning environments where low-level skills using simplified content are the norm. Robert Sternberg, in *Successful Intelligence,* points out that "Fear of failure has been linked to low levels of motivation to achieve." If students are asked to accomplish a set standard in a lock-step, they may be discouraged from accepting and seeking challenge to increase personal levels of accomplishment (1996, p. 262). Students who are protected from falling short in efforts and not expected to spot errors or derive meaning from them have little chance to learn from mistakes. They miss opportunities to examine an approach and discover why it did or did not work and then reevaluate to find a new plan of attack. They are neither forced to collaborate, nor encouraged to look beyond the limits of their own knowledge to solve problems and master concepts. Believing that all wisdom must originate in one's own mind sets one up for disaster sooner or later.

Even if the bar is lowered (see Figure 7.6), there is no guarantee for improved motivation. When falling short of a goal is not equated with failure, however, students may begin to feel comfortable self-choosing projects and goals that are challenging and suited to their learning preferences just to see "if they can do it." And when students self-choose, it means they *want* to tackle the task or the process—they are motivated. Challenging learning environments that *invite* multiple solutions have potentially positive side effects.

CLEAR CRITERIA FOR
DIRECTION AND MASTERY

To provide safe waters for risk taking, especially for open-ended tasks, students must have a general sense of what is expected. It is the framework, the setting of parameters (rituals), mentioned earlier, that sets expectations (see Activity 7.9.). Clear, predefined criteria for mastery give students the yardstick against which ideas and products can be measured. Children can self-evaluate their process, their ideas, and their approach before demonstrating it publicly, knowing every step of the way how they "measure up." In essence, the choices are tailored by the individual to find a comfort level for their own developmental stage and learning preference. "Prove to me that you know this" must be accompanied by clear criteria for judging whether the student *does* know it. "Success," as in Activity 7.9, is not a moving target (see Chapter 9).

Activity 7.9   Vocabulary Teams

Purpose: To teach new vocabulary through an open-ended task, using clear parameters with identifiable criteria as a framework.

Use a 4-day process for teaching new vocabulary by assigning, on day one, a single new vocabulary term to each group of three students. Each group must teach the rest of the class the meaning and spelling of their word. The task is governed by several rules as follows:

- Each group member takes an active role in planning and teaching the new word

- The group presents the new word in written form, correctly spelled and written large enough to be read by all

- The word's meaning must be expressed in two ways other than written language

- Any written language other than the word itself can appear only in speech bubbles; spelling must be correct for words used in them

- The "lesson" must last no longer than 3 minutes

Over the next few days, allow students several 10- to 15-minute work periods to plan songs, poems, raps or rhythm activities, skits, plays, mimes, dances, art work, or cartoons. Allow groups to teach their term, and then stand back and enjoy. The fact that creativity and innovation are welcome (novelty) and nonlinguistic expressions of meaning occur provide challenge to children as they seek to be innovative. Challenge within definite parameters (safety and ritual) makes for a successful lesson. Note: The fact that movement, positive emotion, social interaction, choice, and authentic audiences are integral to this lesson increases the chances that sound memories will be formed—not just of the words children teach, but also of those taught to them. What stimulating and memorable events the lessons become!

8

I've Got It! Now How Do I Keep It?

FACILITATING RECALL

We have seen that rich learning tasks plant rich memories. The more parts of the brain involved in a learning activity, the more likely a strong memory will result. Activities such as Controversy Continuum or Vocabulary Teams are meaningful for the student and require skilled use of content to create a product. They, therefore, are processed throughout the brain, from the cerebral cortex to the primitive regions of the brain. Such tasks are time intensive in the classroom, however, and thus in most instruction are inefficient. Simpler learning activities at times are the most efficient and sensible way to help students *plant* memory.

REVISITATION AND RECALL

An old adage tells us "Practice makes perfect." The simple saying might better read, "Practice makes *easier*." Newly established memory circuits (new synaptic connections) are weak, requiring more energy to fire than established memory circuits. Every time a memory is recalled, neurons in the activated network become more sensitive to the stimulation of adjacent neurons in the firing sequence. They fire *more easily*. So the more frequently one recalls a memory, the easier it is to retrieve it the next time. This gradual easing of effort is apparent with a new phone number; it takes real concentration to remember the numbers initially, but after days and weeks of repeating and writing it, it can be recalled with practically no effort! Activity 8.1 capitalizes on visual stimulation to force memory retrieval.

 Activity 8.1   Key Learning

Purpose: To use icons and visual chunking to represent and rehearse important concepts.

   At the end of a unit of study, after testing is done but before moving on to new instruction, allow students to identify a key learning concept from the completed unit. Use a jigsaw process; each student identifies the one (or two) most meaningful concept(s) he or she learned. Allow only a moment before having the student join a partner to reach consensus on one idea. Continue the jigsaw process by combining two pairs and directing them to reach consensus; then repeat the process by joining more pairs to form groups of 8, then 16, and then the entire class. After the class agrees on one key idea, ask a small committee of students to design a visual icon (no words) to represent the key concept. Upon completion of the icon, have the group explain the icon's message to the class, after which a circle-enclosed icon is mounted high on the wall near the ceiling. The icon will respark the memory of the concept whenever students gaze upon it!

Figure 8.1   Visual Icon

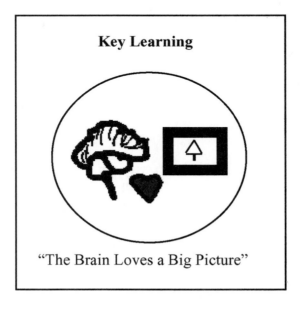

Suggestion: Repeat the key learning activity after each unit of study, adding each new icon to the wall next to the one before it. Eventually, icons will surround the room, and by the end of the year, there will be a visual representation of all key learning that the students themselves selected. Note: The icon committee can be a rotating group to better involve more children in the artistic process.

Declarative/explicit memory circuits must be revisited periodically for a memory circuit to remain viable and "findable." Conversely, if it goes unfired for long enough, the circuit becomes increasingly difficult to retrieve. A person asked to recall a name from 20 years previously might be unable to do so, even with great effort and concentration. But if he or she stumbles on the name while cleaning out old papers, his or her brain will quickly refire the old memory! Periodic, occasional rehearsal improves recall ability.

REPETITION AND PRACTICE

Multiple exposures to a fact or skill do indeed facilitate memory. Years ago, the technique of repeating new learning at specified time intervals became popular. Whole series of instructional materials built on a spiraling, a repeat of concepts over time, are successful today (i.e., Saxon Math and Daily Oral Language).

Recent research bears out the effectiveness of repetition. Students need to revisit and practice new material often and over an extended period of time in order to do more than just parrot back details (Marzano, Pickering, & Pollock, 2001). A student must be able to recall a concept as a first step toward using it in a meaningful fashion—whether in practical application or higher level synthesis. Activity 8.2 includes a number of possibilities.

 Activity 8.2   Repetition Routines

Purpose: To build quick, frequent opportunities for rehearsal of material into instruction.

Whenever appropriate, provide means for students to practice concepts. Several activities which can become classroom rituals include the following:

(Continued)

Activity 8.2 (continued)

- Have students repeat back important concepts to your prompts. It should be done several times, until the class answers boldly, attentively, and in unison.

- After delivering instruction or reviewing ideas, pause for a brief period and ask students to turn to a neighbor close to them: Have them tell each other what they heard you say. (Not only does revisitation and repetition occur but there is also movement, change of state to maintain attention, social interaction, and opportunities for students to clarify misunderstandings that their peers may have. It is safer for a duo to ask for clarification and explanation following the share time if both are confused than for an individual student to voice questions!)

- Ask students to create songs, poems, or raps about some area of study, incorporating, perhaps, at least five facts.

Encourage students to prepare a "cheat sheet" for an upcoming quiz. Limit the sheet size, and let them fit as many facts as they can on it. Debrief the items for "cheating" on an overhead transparency by asking students to share what they have included on their cheat sheets. Have them record on the transparency until space is used up. Students can add new ideas to their own sheets from the class debrief. This is a great review process: Students revisit their notes once to create their original sheet (a product not likely to result if you just ask them to review by "looking over" their notes) and are exposed to review a second time as they say the items, a third time when they are recorded via the projector, and a fourth time when they peruse their sheet for the test. Review, review, review.

- Do a Prediction Game, where students write answers to questions and small groups within the classroom work to construct the correct corresponding questions. (This forces children to revisit notes or text, plus discuss concepts.)

- Ask students to record four dynamite ideas from instruction on a note card and then circulate throughout the classroom to borrow two additional, new ideas from classmates. Repeat again until each child has eight new facts or concepts written down.

- Follow-up: Have students create a "slot" book to highlight the eight ideas with illustrations or explanations, if appropriate (see Figure 8.2). Suggestion: Collect all booklets, and return them to students after a week to serve as one additional exposure to concepts—or send them home to be shared with family members.

Figure 8.2 Slot Book

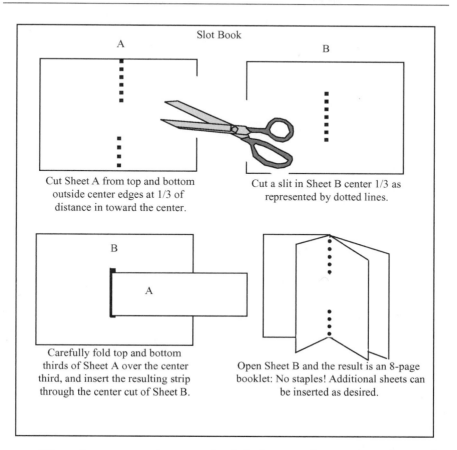

Slot Book

A

B

Cut Sheet A from top and bottom outside center edges at 1/3 of distance in toward the center.

Cut a slit in Sheet B center 1/3 as represented by dotted lines.

B

A

Carefully fold top and bottom thirds of Sheet A over the center third, and insert the resulting strip through the center cut of Sheet B.

Open Sheet B and the result is an 8-page booklet: No staples! Additional sheets can be inserted as desired.

- Place key concepts on colorful sheets of paper, and cut the paper into unusual shapes to create pieces as for a jigsaw puzzle. Hand out one set to each group of three to four students, and have them reform the puzzle and then share out the concept on their group "puzzle."

- Challenge Cards: When children return to class the day following new instruction, group them in triads immediately. Give each group a Challenge Card containing a question on the content from the day before. Provide limited time (no more than 3 minutes) to find the correct answer to the question, using any source of information within the classroom necessary (textbook, memory, notes, another group, a fellow student, or the teacher). Groups report out their question and correct responses in a whole-class, fast-paced debrief. The entire class verifies the correctness of each response and then chorales responses in unison. Not only is this an enjoyable and safe review, it

(Continued)

Activity 8.2 (continued)

is faster than a whole-class, teacher-led question-and-answer session. Follow-up: Re-collect cards, shuffle them, and hand them out again and see if the class can beat the previous time.

- For sequenced items, write each step in the sequence on a separate card. String a line across some portion of the classroom, and clothespin each card on the line in an incorrect order. Have students rearrange them correctly. Repeat periodically, until the correct sequence is mastered.

- Round-robin reviews can occur at the end of the class period. Before dismissing, ask students "What did you learn today?" Ask students to work in pairs to respond, with this rule: Each pair must contribute an idea, but with *no* repeats.

Multiple exposures to concepts increase the likelihood of learning. Learning can be increased 47.9% when a student is exposed to four practice sessions. Yet to increase learning to close to 80% of full mastery, children need 24 practice sessions! (Anderson, 1995; Newell & Rosenbloom, 1981, as quoted in Marzano, Pickering, & Pollock, 2001). (See Activity 8.3.)

 Activity 8.3   Note Chart

Purpose: To help students review through a note-taking and study strategy.

Model for students a note-taking and study strategy. Using a passage of written text or an instructional videotape, ask students to write down as much of what they hear as possible in the right-hand side of a note form given to them (see Figure 8.3, column B). Once complete, model for students the identification of key words or phrases most indicative of the spirit of the recorded information. Next, ask students to lift those identified words or phrases and record them in column A, next to the corresponding section of notes from which they were taken in column B.

Using a piece of scrap paper to cover column B, ask students to rely on key terms in column A to recall as much detail as possible from the notes. Students can self-check by rereading the full notes in the right-hand column.

Figure 8.3   Note Organizer

Keys	Notes
3 types of rocks igneous metamorphic sedimentary	There are three basic types of rocks. Igneous rocks are formed under intense heat, and often result from volcanic eruptions. Basalt is a good example of this type of rock, looking much like black glass when it is mined. Metamorphic rocks are those that change form, perhaps through pressure or heat, particularly when the rock hardens. One type of metamorphic rock that has a shining reputation is a diamond, so compressed that it becomes crystalline. The third type of rock is sedimentary, getting its name by the process which forms it. When matter settles to the bottom of a liquid or settles out of ice or the air, such as sand does, it can compress and dry to form layered rocks.

Content visited too infrequently or in isolation from practical application might be recallable for only short periods of time. To ensure more than superficial understanding, memory planting should include a variety of activities to appeal to all learning styles, plus the use of content in some meaningful fashion, as evidenced in tasks in Activity 8.4. Repetition, repetition, repetition.

Ideally, the practice tasks should occur frequently, allowing no more than 2 days to pass from original instruction before revisiting a concept that is to be committed to memory. Because initial learning may be "soft"

✳ **Activity 8.4**   Geography Circles
_____

Purpose: To acclimate students to geographic locations of states and give practice in map directions.

Pass out maps of the entire country of study, with state/province boundaries marked and major cities located. After students learn names and locations of the states, provide them with compasses to use for measurement of miles per map scale from given points: For example, have children draw a circle with a specified radius, say 500 miles, from the city of Boise, Idaho (or, e.g., St. Louis, Missouri). Ask students what direction they would have to travel in to pass through the greatest number of different states and to name the states in the order they would be crossed. Repeat either by randomly naming distances and cities or by drawing mile numbers and city names from a bowl. Variations:

- (1) Create mini-mysteries to inspire student work. "The suspect traveled five hundred eighty miles out of a city with a population greater than one million, yet still had not crossed the state line. In what state could he be?" (2) Ask children to create a mileage chart for the Midwestern states between all cities with populations in excess of 100,000.

---

and fragile (and fleeting in its capacity for retrieval), long-term storage of memory might be thought of as "hard" wiring. Much of the transfer from the soft easy-triggered cells to the hard storage cells for long lasting memory must be done with repetition (Medina, Repa, Mauk, & LeDoux, 2002). That translates into spiraling of curriculum, manipulation, review, and revisitation over time. The more often memories are recalled (practiced), the easier and more automatic retrieval becomes. There is less need for frontal lobe processing to perform or recall: The automaticity (or developed procedural memory) takes over and makes refiring of memory easier.

When concepts are mastered, they shouldn't be shelved just because the unit of study is "marked off the list." Take opportunities to refresh concepts learned in the past. Otherwise, older memories (even those soundly planted) will get increasingly harder to retrieve, eventually even being discarded. A brain intent on maintaining the useful and eliminating the frivolous is proof of the adage, "Use it or lose it." Remember: Academic learning is meant to prepare children for life, not for the classroom or the chapter test. If children learn only to forget later, then the only real use content has is for test or quiz performance. No deep pool of retrievable memory exists for improvisation and problem solving outside of the classroom; no brain is empowered.

Maximize learning for your students by growing their brains through sound instruction; then ensure that memory is rehearsed enough to be retrievable. If learning is *change*, then practice makes that change permanent.

9

Hey, How Am I Doing?

Feedback in the Learning Process

Nothing happens until something moves.

—Albert Einstein, 1879–1955

We have seen that the brain makes sense of new experiences by comparing them to the old. It draws on successful past behavior to strategize for the present. If it is easier for a student to solve a long-addition problem using graph paper to keep the digits straight, he or she will take care to align digits before tackling his or her first long-division problem to avoid error. The road to understanding and response is not straight and the process is not like switching on a light bulb—click and there is understanding. No, it requires trial and error, starts and stops, speedups and slowdowns—and lots of tweaking. It requires learning what works and what does not.

Learning is change and so involves uncertainty. Learners perceive, emote, sort, act, and measure to determine if their actions are appropriate to a situation. Therefore, students need feedback to gauge progress toward mastery, and it should be present in each step of instruction. When performance falls short of an expected stage of mastery, students should be given opportunities to continue work or rework until they succeed. Achievement seems to improve when they do (Marzano, Pickering, & Pollock, 2001). Corrective feedback and teacher support help children plan, persevere, and deal with the complexity of tasks.

FEEDBACK AND ASSESSMENT

The focus of this chapter is the importance of assessment and feedback *in the learning process*. It is the term *feedback* that best encompasses the spirit of maximized learning that *Blueprint for Student Success* is targeting. According to the *Random House Webster's School & Office Dictionary*, feedback is "a reaction or a response." It can be as subtle as a nod or as overt as a red-ink letter grade on a final exam. But in academic settings, it serves as communication concerning progress toward mastery in learning.

In truly effective instruction, feedback opportunities are interspersed throughout tasks at times and in ways that are appropriate: Students need to master the concept of equations before they are ready to work on algebraic algorithms. So feedback to students and teachers alike is essential before scaffolding to a higher level. Each step, each fundamental, each brick in the foundation of learning requires some sort of feedback to measure readiness to move on and help the student confidently and accurately create new meaning. Feedback must answer "How am I doing?"

If feedback is a reaction or response to an activity, assessment judges the value of the accomplishment. The Educators in Connecticut Pomperaug Regional School District 15 (1996) in *Performance-Based Learning and Assessment* define it as the collection of data about student performance. Either the assessment indicates areas of strength and weakness or defines the general level of the quality of work. The latter implies academic evaluation of mastery, an interim or final measure in a completed process. Both are critically important for learning and must be built into instruction.

Enhancing Achievement

"The most powerful single modification to enhance achievement is feedback," according to John. A. Hattie (Marzano et al., 2001, p. 96). Close supervision with feedback ensures that

- New concepts are accurately perceived
- Progress in acquiring identified knowledge is steady
- Mastery is complete

Surely, feedback should not only be broad in its application but also multipurposed. It is used as an evaluation of whether content has been successfully memorized, as a tool for accountability (for grading students), and as a way to distribute learning opportunities. Yet its primary purpose must serve to keep students on track toward mastery.

Considerations for Feedback

To be most effective, feedback must be both timely and corrective. If administered too soon, it is not optimal; given too late, and it is without value. Students need to know not only *if* their work is correct or incorrect but also why. If errors exist, students should be made to correct them after explanation and discussion. At least a day should pass after initial instruction before testing for mastery to allow the brain to retrace a new memory circuit and firmly plant the memory network for recall. The brain needs time to fire and retrace new connections and establish new learning for later recall (much of this is during REM sleep). Of course, if too much time passes and a memory is not revisited, it can be lost. Thus, prudent use of practice to plant memory and careful timing of feedback assessments can facilitate student success (see tasks in Activity 9.1).

 Activity 9.1   Staggered Feedback

Purpose: To provide ample feedback en route to mastery while timing summative assessment for optimum results.

• Provide instruction on concepts, perhaps science terms such as *deciduous* and *evergreen*. Ask students to define the terms (to provide feedback to the teacher regarding foundational knowledge, preinstruction). Next, direct students to test the accuracy of their definitions by referencing a dictionary or text glossary or by listening to direct instruction or video narration.

• Discuss, whole class, whether any perceptions regarding the terms have changed. Ask students to record information they have discovered concerning the new terms in a journal.

• Pair classmates and have them compare their respective journal entries, reconciling their ideas to ensure accuracy and thoroughness.

• Assign homework: Locate and sketch in journals one example each of a deciduous and an evergreen tree. The trees must be off school property.

- Share out all discoveries with partners the next class period and follow up with a quick peer assessment of homework examples. Children will be ready to share with the entire class their example choices.

- Debrief the entire class, sharing examples and answering remaining questions.

- For a final assessment, have students take a 10-minute field trip to the lawn area of the school. Have students find and sketch an example of each type of tree and write an explanation as to why it fits the chosen category. Note: Feedback is given before, during, and after instruction, along with ample opportunities for self-correction en route to mastery. The final assessment is given at least 1 day after delivery of direct instruction.

Deciding What to Evaluate

Clear identification of learning goals and establishment of criteria for mastery of those goals must precede the planning of any learning task. Failure to do so tends to result in activity-driven instruction rather than instruction that focuses on critical content and skills. When goals drive assessments, poor assessments based on criteria unrelated to lesson goals can be eliminated: Correct spelling, for instance, should not be a criterion for expressing understanding of a math algorithm unless the lesson is an interdisciplinary one focusing also on the mechanics of writing.

A unit on the Civil War can have as a goal the mastery of major concepts pertaining to causes of social, economic, and civil upheaval rather than lists of details—unless the goal is to ready students for a popular trivia game. Instruction should not be "List the three events, in order, that started the Civil War" (simple recall, and all lower level skills) but rather "How could the economic, political, or social concerns of the South have been met to save the Union without war?"

Such an assessment question requires students to comprehend, recall, and manipulate information—and then reason and problem solve. It is open ended, as it invites multiple answers. Since there is no single correct answer, it invites creativity and choice in decision making and requires a display of understanding of interconnected circumstances in real-life events. Solving today's political dilemmas requires creative thinking and problem solving as does solving problems from any other era in history: So to better equip our students for citizenship, they need practice in such skills. (Along the way, it might even be more interesting than memorizing the three of this, the five of that, the two causes, the fourteen reasons . . . yawn.

Figure 9.1 Aligning Components of a Learning Activity

Lesson Goals Identified	Criteria for Mastery Identified	Assessments Determined	Lesson Activities
• depict relationship among facts and concepts (science) in preparation for writing project	• able to successfully extract and organize key information from written text • able to transpose key concepts and relationships between them to outline form	• student creation of concept map to express understanding of ideas/info • student-created outline, with all major points and subpoints concerning a concept (i.e., photosynthesis)	• model note-taking: students practice, feedback given and corrections made • instruct children in use of concept map: teacher models using materials from notes • children create concept map on another topic from written text • teacher debrief of concept maps: children self assess • use concept maps to identify key and subordinate points: teacher models outlining. • student outlining of concept map provided by teacher

Wonder why undermotivated kids might opt for something other than preparing for that test?)

Every stage of the learning process requires assessments of progress: learning levels and readiness prior to instruction, progress and understanding during it, and measurement of the degree of mastery as a culmination to the instructional unit.

FEEDBACK FOR TEACHING DECISIONS

Instruction improves when strengths and weaknesses of students are diagnosed prior to beginning a unit of study. Identifying the preexisting knowledge of students can help to better plan instruction. The teacher can identify deficiencies in foundational skills that must be in place before introducing new content, determine sound approaches for helping students make new connections, and indicate proper pacing for instruction.

Preinstruction monitoring can be accomplished through teacher observation, interviews, surveys and self-evaluation by the students, checklists, and student think-alouds, as well as through multiple-choice or short-answer pretests (see Chapter 1, Activities 1.1 and 1.2). Activity 9.2 provides a safe method for monitoring student understanding.

 Activity 9.2   Passing Packets

Purpose: To gain preinstruction feedback on key topics or concepts through a safe, interactive task.

• Place students in groups of 4. Number the groups for identification. Prepare and hand out one file folder for each group of children that contains as many sheets as there are groups in the class (e.g., a classroom of 28 students would require 7 sheets per folder). Each file folder contains a different term or question based on a key concept about to be taught in a unit of study. Seven groups would necessitate 7 different terms or concepts for consideration.

• Instruct groups to open the file folder they have been given and then read and discuss the question or term on the sheet that corresponds to their group number. The group responds through consensus if possible but is also invited to enter observations or reactions to the sheet term. Give students a fixed amount of time to work, perhaps 2 minutes. Repeat the process, passing the folders in a round-robin fashion until all file folders (and terms) have circulated to all tables.

(Continued)

Activity 9.2 (continued)

- Exchange folders one more time, randomly. Each group then opens the completed packet to read, discuss, and compile the most significant reflections for the file folder concept.

- Chart and discuss the selections with the whole class. Good debate might occur, questions might arise, and interests might be sparked. Set recorded ideas aside and refer to them as instruction—and discovery of concepts—unfolds.

- *Replicate the process at the end of instruction.* Encourage children to compare the preinstruction responses to those of postinstruction. Students will discover their thinking has changed and see their own growth. It is tangible proof that they have truly learned!

Teachers need to assess that which the children already know and understand before starting new instruction, because the accuracy of preconceived notions colors how new information fits into one's overall concept of the world. It would be unthinkable to teach a person the rules of the road if he or she had never been in an automobile. Likewise, it is foolhardy to teach multiplication to a child who has yet to master plain addition!

The most common (albeit overused) means for establishing prior knowledge is to ask children what they already know about a topic and then what they would *like* to learn about it—before instruction begins. In this process (often nicknamed KWL, for **k**now/**w**ant to know/have **l**earned), students revisit what they learned after a unit of instruction is over to determine if all their queries (preinstruction) were answered.

Such an activity helps students tie new concepts with prior knowledge (see Chapter 5). But overuse and sole use of such a method limits children's arena of curiosity. It is unlikely that a classroom of learners will probe sophisticated topics and ponder exciting possibilities about a concept. After all, when children are asked to identify what they *want* to know, they don't know it yet! How do children know what they want to know, when they don't know it yet? A bigger bag of tools affords improved opportunities for tapping prior knowledge. (See Activity 9.3.)

 Activity 9.3   Throw a Thought

Purpose: To provide a safe means of tapping into individual ideas before the onset of instruction and to gauge student readiness for new instruction.

Ask students to respond to a major concept that will be targeted in upcoming instruction: for instance, "Why is it hotter in July than it is in January?" Putting no identifying marks on the written responses, have students crumple their papers into a wad and toss them into the center of the classroom floor or into a large box or bucket. When instructed to do so, students each pick up one wadded paper, open it, and read it. Place students in triads and ask them to discuss the ideas on the papers they have retrieved and the merits or problems or significance of them. After just a few moments, redirect student attention to whole-class activity. Ask students to report out the ideas on the papers—and their reactions to them. Record any concerns, questions, or points of disagreement, such as "Things We Need to Find Out." Not only does the teacher gain an understanding of student perceptions, children have a benchmark from which to begin their studies—and potentially some self-identified questions to answer as instruction unfolds.

TRACKING STUDENT PROGRESS

Feedback must also be embedded within instruction to properly monitor and measure the *progress* of learning (see Activity 9.4). Continuous monitoring of student thinking and skill enables a teacher to identify if a student needs further clarification, extra practice, or individualized attention. Materials can be retaught or represented in a way that gives youngsters additional opportunities for mastery, and student self-assessment can provide chances to self-correct. This is evidenced in Activity 9.5.

 Activity 9.4   Feedback Grab Bag

Purpose: To embed feedback in instruction for monitoring progress in a variety of ways.

Expose students to variety in feedback measures beyond matching, true–false and multiple-choice assessments.

Teachers can measure the progress of learning by

- Monitoring student reflections and journal entries
- Observing student responses or performance, with documentation
- Examining portfolios
- Oral questioning or interview

(Continued)

Activity 9.4 (continued)

- Observing student think-alouds
- Viewing learning logs
- Conferencing with students
- Evaluating products
- Examining student-generated illustrations or visual organizers

Students can self-assess and self-monitor progress or thoroughness using

- Checklists
- Guided self-assessment tools which list elements to indicate excellence (e.g., "Did I use a capital letters to begin the sentence?" or "Did I use estimation to check the likelihood of correct results of my multiplication?")
- Making midstream or final rubric checks
- Comparing personal work to exemplars which serve as yardsticks for comparison
- Comparing their classwork or homework against whole-class examples given during debriefs and discussions
- Comparing their process/product to that modeled by the teacher
- Examining sequenced portfolio entries

Note: Peer sharing can also provide constructive evaluation for improvement or change. Possibilities include use of criteria checklists as guides for peer feedback and peer collaboration on product/process assessment lists.

Note: Great sources for assessment and feedback possibilities include Lewin and Shoemaker's (1998) *Great Performances: Creating Classroom-Based Assessment Tasks* and The Educators in Connecticut's Pomperaug Regional School District 15's (1996) *A Teacher's Guide to Performance-Based Learning and Assessment* (see References and Resources).

 Activity 9.5   Moving Handoff

Purpose: To provide a safe method for giving and receiving feedback regarding newly learned content.

- Give each student a 4" × 5" card, and ask them to mark one Side A and one Side B. Provide two questions from material recently taught to students, one identified as Question A and one as Question B.

- Instruct the youngsters to answer each question on the designated side of the card by recording responses in any means they want, as long as they communicate clearly, using words, icons, visual representations, or webs. No names or identifying marks that would reveal the author should be put on the card.

- Tell children that they have only a few minutes to record their ideas. Once they hear music begin playing, they are to stop recording and begin to move around the classroom. As long as music is playing, they exchange the card in their possession over and over again.

- When the music stops, have children freeze silently in position until new directions are given. At that point, ask students to pair with the person closest to them physically at that moment. Allow no foot movement, only turning or twisting their bodies, to face their new partner (this guarantees that new partnerships are formed and that no one is left out).

- Instruct each student to read the card he or she holds and then to share the ideas on it with his or her partner. They can spot confusions, check accuracy, debate ideas, and validate answers.

- Follow the pair-sharing with a whole-class discussion, where students report their findings. In the process, they review accurate concepts, correct misconceptions, detect omissions, etc. A great review, as well as a safe manner to assess the understanding and performance of others: as a yardstick to measuring one's own.

Note: This process is a great one for controversial issues, where anonymity is essential in both communicating ideas and expressing judgment about the ideas of others.

Awareness of how well one is learning compared to others is not critically important to a learner, and in fact can become an exercise in ranking students that leads to competition. Feedback is meant to aid the individual on his learning journey by measuring progress toward a *standard*, constantly reassessing the game plan for mastery. Criterion-based and diagnostic feedback guides student learning, making that student an active participant, and not a pawn, in the process.[1] Absence of opportunities for correction and redirection in the midst of a learning activity equates to failed teaching.

Feedback tools, therefore, must be interspersed throughout the instruction. They cannot be used solely as end-of-instruction summative assessments where a child is judged as having succeeded or failed at mastery. If one truly believes that all children can learn, then ongoing opportunities must be provided for each child to reach academic standards regardless of his or her learning preferences or ability level. A student who falls short is not "off the hook," but with guidance is expected to reassess efforts, examine reasons for falling short, and consider alternative approaches to mastery. Youngsters will learn perseverance and gain confidence for reaching academic goals in the future.

DETERMINING MASTERY

Some feedback evaluates a product or process rather than straight content, assessing whether students have mastered application of particular skills or content at higher levels of thinking. Marzano, Bond, Herman, and Arter (1994) divides outcomes into two categories: process skills and content/ declarative knowledge skills. Content/declarative knowledge involves such things as recalling facts (like dates or events); multiple-choice and short-answer assessments are adequate to measure mastery.

But when complex process skills are assessed, the assessment requires more of a performance, as in Activity 9.6. Such assessments might include concept mapping; writing tasks; problem solving; setting up experiments; critical thinking tasks; group cooperation; concept application in higher level thinking; or performances as in dance, music, or sports. They measure the products of student learning.

 Activity 9.6   Concept Map Assessment

Purpose: To assess student understanding of concepts and their interrelationships in a visual fashion.

After children are familiar with concept mapping, ask them to use concept mapping to express understanding of content or process. Rather than using written explanations, ask students to map a concept (perhaps the water cycle, seed classification, the relationship of characters in literature, or the history of California). When used preinstruction, it clearly reveals prior knowledge, shallow understanding or misunderstandings, gaps in knowledge, or improper reasoning. In the midst of instruction, it can monitor developing connections and accuracy in perceptions. Used postinstruction as a summative assessment, it can evaluate a student's overall level of mastery (see Figure 5.3). A concept map can also be used both pre- and postinstruction to provide great visual feedback for students to gauge personal growth and learning. Note: Good resources on concept mapping and visual organizers are David Hyerle's (1996, 2000) *A Field Guide to using Visual Tools* and *Visual Tools for Constructing Knowledge* and Buzan and Buzan's (1996) *The Mind Map Book: How to Use Radiant Thinking to Maximize Your Brain's Untapped Potential.*

For measurement of such complex procedural skills, assessment tasks should require the students to use the targeted skills and measure them against criteria of successful performance. If the lesson goal is about improved visual or verbal communication, then impact on the audience rather than isolated qualities such as volume should be the primary consideration. Can the speaker be heard? Do illustrations relate the key concepts of the text? Criteria should involve the knowledge of the content, the quality of the product or how well the work was presented in the mandated format, and the quality of the application (Marzano et al., 1994).

Whenever using rubrics and exemplars, make certain students know

1. The standard, skill, or content they are working toward: "What does it look like?"

2. How they will be assessed: "What end product is expected?"

3. Which criteria will be used for measurement: "What are the features and characteristics of excellence?"

With such clear guidelines, the assessment process pits the student product against the evaluation tool and not against the teacher. Figure 9.2 demonstrates a defined evaluation tool with clear guidelines. Children can self-evaluate to spot their errors and then fine-tune to hit the target. The target is not moving, as the yardstick for excellence is unchanging. Each child must know what excellence looks like, and there must be feedback and guidance along the way for the student to achieve it.

FEEDBACK FOR MOTIVATION AND STUDENT ACCOUNTABILITY

"Along the way . . ." is key. Learners need *ongoing* and *multiple* forms of feedback. I have known teachers who, at the midterm point of a grading period, discover they have provided no feedback to students or received any from them to judge student progress toward mastery. Disaster hits when a final test indicates failure. If schools existed primarily for the purpose of sorting and funneling youth into appropriate pathways at a given moment in time, then snapshot assessments would be all the accountability needed. But if we are to empower these young folks, we need to make them—and us—accountable for their learning the entire journey through.

That is possible in an environment with no academic secrets: one that is full of opportunity to self-assess and full of awareness of solid, identified criteria and standards. The opportunities for monitoring might be as simple as charting their own increasing accuracy and speed in performing multiplication tables. It could be using visual organizers to self-check their identification of adjectives in a seat-work task over parts of speech. But if children

Figure 9.2

	Focus	Elaboration	Organization	Integration
6	• My story flowed smoothly from beginning to end. • I had a great closing. • I wrote about only one event. • I included reactions that make sense.	• I explained the event by using specific details and examples, although some of my episodes and reactions may be better developed than others. • I told how I felt about the examples and how this event affected my life. • I used descriptive words to tell my story.	• I used all paragraphs appropriately. • I wrote a clear narrative that moves through time without gaps. • I used different kinds of sentences so that my sentences are related to each other (cohesion). • All of my transitions connect my story from beginning to end (coherence).	• My story was easy to understand. • All the details of my story were connected together. • My story was outstanding in all areas.
5	• Most of my story flowed from beginning to end. • I wrote about my feelings throughout the paper. • Most of the reactions I included make sense. • I had a closing.	• I told how I felt during the event. • I used some descriptive words to tell my story. • I explained this event by using some specific details and examples.	• I wrote a narrative that moves through time with few gaps. • Most of the episodes are appropriately paragraphed. • I used some different kinds of sentences to tie the story together (cohesion). • I used some different transition words to tie my ideas and paragraphs together (coherence).	• My story had some details and made sense. • Some parts of my paper are better developed than others.
4	• My story was clear, and I stayed on track. • I knew how I felt about the event and wrote some things about it. • My paper has reactions, but some may not be stated directly in the paper. • I might not have a closing.	• I told about some things that happened during the event using specific details. • I need more development of depth. • I told how I felt during the event.	• My narrative had a beginning, middle, and end. • I used some appropriate paragraphing of the episodes (coherence). • I used some simple transitions that help tell the story events (coherence).	• My story was simple and clear.

3	• My story was clear, but I got off track. • I forgot to tell how I felt about the topic. • I needed more details. • I did not include reactions, or my reactions did not make sense. • I may not have written enough.	• My story had a few general details and examples. • I included only a list of episodes or reactions. • I may not have written enough.	• I wrote a narrative, but there were gaps in the story. • Some of my paragraphs are inappropriate. • My paper may include transitions that are confusing. • I may not have written enough.	• I started my story, but left out some important details.
2	• My story was not clear. • I forgot to write about my reactions and feelings. • I needed to write more and put it in good order. • I did not write a story that moved through time. • I did not write enough.	• I needed more parts to my story, and they needed to be connected. • I may not have written a narrative paper. • I did not include appropriate paragraphing. • I did not write enough.	• I may not have written a narrative • My sentences were not clear. • I did not write enough.	• I tried to follow the directions, but big parts were missing.
1	• I did not write about the story.	• I needed to write a story and include details.	• I did not write a narrative. • I did not write enough.	• I did not follow the directions. • I needed to write more.

CONVENTIONS

2	• I have mastered sentence construction. • My paper may have a few invented spellings of uncommon words. • Subjects and their verbs agree correctly. • My paper has demonstrated mastery of basic punctuation and capitalization.	1	• The number of errors in my paper interferes with my readers' understanding.

Reprinted with permission from the Illinois State Board of Education.

SOURCE: Reprinted with permission from the Illinois State Board of Education.

125

know at any given time where they are on the road to the performance goal, there will more likelihood of intrinsic motivation. Intrinsic motivation increases when one has higher personal stakes in the outcome (Marzano et al., 2001).

Motivation suffers when students perceive assessments as hurdles rather than fair measures or as limits rather than possibilities. When obscure details or unimportant trivia drive assessments and demands for replication have no purpose other than for rote recall, a struggling student might simply give up—while the high-ability child might still be unchallenged. If we want all students to successfully meet our curriculum standards, all students—not just the "crème de la crème"—must be *able* to prove mastery. Baseline learning should be accompanied by invitations to levels beyond those expected of every child through challenging, choice-filled tasks that allow demonstration of mastery for all.

Educators must continually seek ways to maximize learning for each and every child. An integral part of instructional delivery—feedback—plays a fundamental role in doing just that. It's not the sprinkles, not the icing, but the glue that holds together the entire learning experience!

NOTE

1   Measures a student's performance against some targeted level of mastery.

References

Anderson, J. R. (1995). *Learning and memory: An integrated approach.* New York: Wiley.

Aurelius, A. (1909–14). *The Harvard classics: The meditations of Marcus Aurelius* (Vol. II, Part 3, George Long, Trans.). New York: Collier.

Bartlett, J. (1983). Bartlett's *Familiar quotations.* Minneapolis: Econo-Clad Books.

Beane, J. A., & Lipka, R. P. (1986). *Self-concept, self esteem and the curriculum.* New York: Teachers College Press.

Binet, A., & Simon, T. (1916). *The development of intelligence in children.* Baltimore: Williams & Wilkins. (Reprinted 1973, New York: Arno Press; 1983, Salem, NH: Ayer.)

Blake, W. (1790-93). *The marriage of Heaven and Hell.* London: Dent.

Bloom, B. S. (1956). *Taxonomy of educational objectives (cognitive domain).* New York: Longman.

Branden, N. (1987). *How to raise your self-esteem.* New York: Bantam.

Branden, N. (1994). *Six pillars of self-esteem.* New York: Bantam.

Brewer, C., & Campbell, D. G. (1991). *Rhythms of learning.* Tucson, AZ: Zephyr Press.

Bruer, J. T. (1999). *Schools for thought: A science of learning in the classroom.* Cambridge: MIT Press.

Buzan, T., & Buzan, B. (1996). *The mind map book: How to use radiant thinking to maximize your brain's untapped potential.* New York: Plume.

Caine, G., Caine, R. N., & Crowell, S. (1994). *Mindshifts.* Tucson, AZ: Zephyr Press.

Caine, R. N., & Caine, G. (1997a). *Education on the edge of possibility.* Alexandria, VA: Association for Supervision and Curriculum Development.

Caine, R. N., & Caine, G. (1997b). *Unleashing the power of perceptual change: The potential of brain-based teaching.* Alexandria, VA: Association for Supervision and Curriculum Development.

Calhoun, E. F. (1999). *Teaching beginning reading and writing.* Alexandria, VA: Association for Supervision and Curriculum Development.

Calvin, W. H. (1996). *How brains think.* New York: Basic.

Carroll, L. (1872). *Through the looking glass.*

Costa, A. L., & Kallick, B. (2000). *Habits of mind: Activating and engaging habits of mind.* Alexandria, VA: Association for Supervision and Curriculum Development.

Coué, É. (1922). *Self-mastery through conscious autosuggestion.* Kila, MT: Kessinger.

Csikszentmihalyi, M. (1997). *Creativity: Flow and the psychology of discovery and invention.* New York: HarperCollins.

Diamond, M., & Hopson, J. (1998). *Magic trees of the mind.* New York: Penguin Putnam.

Educators in Connecticut's Pomperaug Regional School District 15 (1996). *A teacher's guide to performance-based learning and assessment.* Alexandria, VA: Association for Supervision and Curriculum Development.

Engel, A. K., Fries, P., & Singer, W. (2001). Dynamic predictions: Oscillations and synchrony in top-down processing. *Nature Reviews Neuroscience, 2,* 704-716.

Gagne, R. (1985*). The conditions of learning* (4th ed.). New York: Holt, Rinehart & Winston.

Gardner, H. (1991). *The unschooled mind: How children think and how schools should teach.* New York: Basic.

Gardner, H. (1997). *Extraordinary minds.* New York: Basic.

George, J. C. (1974). *Julie of the wolves.* New York: Harper Trophy.

Goleman, D. (1995). *Emotional intelligence.* New York: Bantam.

Hannaford, C. (1995). *Smart moves.* Arlington, VA: Great Ocean.

Hyerle, D. (1996). *Visual tools for constructing knowledge.* Alexandria, VA: Association for Supervision and Curriculum Development.

Hyerle, D. (2000). *A field guide to using visual tools.* Alexandria, VA: Association for Supervision and Curriculum Development.

Illinois State Board of Education. (2002). *Illinois Standards Achievement Test: Sample Writing Handbook 2002: Grades 3, 5, and 8.* Springfield: Author.

Jensen, A. R. (1998). *The "g" factor: The science of mental ability, human evolution, behavior, and intelligence.* Westport, CT: Praeger.

Jensen, E. (1995). *Brain-based learning and teaching.* Del Mar, CA: Turning Point.

Jensen, E. (1996). *Cerebral showcase.* Del Mar, CA: Turning Point.

Joyce, J. (1922). *Ulysses.* Paris: Sylvia Beach Shakespeare & Company.

LeDoux, J. (1996). *The emotional brain.* New York: Simon & Schuster.

Lewin, L., & Shoemaker, B. J. (1998). *Great performances: Creating classroom-based assessment tasks.* Alexandria, VA: Association for Supervision and Curriculum Development.

Lou, Y., Abrami, P. C., Spence, J. C., Paulsen, C., Chambers, B., & d'Apollonio, S. (1996). Within-class grouping: A meta-analysis. *Review of Educational Research, 66*(4), 423-458.

Mann, L. (2000). Recalculating middle school math. *Association for Supervision and Curriculum Development Education Update, 42*(1), 1-2, 8.

Martin, D. J. (1997). *Elementary science methods: A constructivist approach.* New York: Delmar.

Marzano, R., Bond, L., Herman, J., & Arter, J. (1994). *Supporting educational improvement with alternative assessment readings: Laboratory Network Program Alternative Assessment Toolkit* (p.15). Portland, OR: Northwest Regional Educational Laboratory.

Marzano, R. J., Pickering, D. J., & Pollock, J. E. (2001). *Classroom instruction that works.* Alexandria, VA: Association for Supervision and Curriculum Development.

Medina, J. F., Repa, J. C., Mauk, M. D., & LeDoux, J. E (2002). Parallels between cerebellum- and amygdala-dependent conditioning. *Nature Reviews Neuroscience, 3,* 122-131.

Newell, A., & Rosenbloom, P. S. (1981). Mechanisms of skill acquisition and the law of practice. In J. R. Anderson (Ed.), *Cognitive skills and their acquisition.* Hillsdale, NJ: Lawrence Erlbaum.

Patton, G. S. (1947). *War as I knew it.* New York: Houghton Mifflin.

Peoples, D. A. (1992). *Presentations plus.* New York: Wiley.

Perkins, D. (1992). *Smart Schools: Better thinking and learning for every child.* New York: Free Press.

Perkins, D. (1995). *Outsmarting IQ: The emerging science of learnable intelligence.* New York: Free Press.

Piaget, J. (1923). *The origin of intelligence in children.*

Ratey, J. J. (2001). *A user's guide to the brain.* New York: Pantheon.

Sechenov, I. M. (1863). *Reflexes of the brain.*

Sousa, D. A. (2001). *How the brain learns.* Thousand Oaks, CA: Corwin.

Sternberg, R. J. (1996). *Successful intelligence.* New York: Simon & Schuster.

Swartz, B., & Parks, S. (1994). *Infusing the teaching of critical and creative thinking into elementary instruction: A lesson design handbook.* St. Augustine, FL: Critical Thinking.

Sylwester, R. (1995). *A celebration of neurons: An educator's guide to the human brain.* Alexandria, VA: ASCD.

Sylwester, R. (2000). *A biological brain in a cultural classroom.* Thousand Oaks, CA: Corwin.

United State Fish and Wildlife Services, Minnesota Valley National Wildlife Refuge (2002). *Habitats as homes.* Bloomington, MN: Author.

Waelti, P., Dickenson, A., & Schultz, W. (2001). Dopamine responses comply with basic assumptions of formal learning theory. *Nature 412,* 43-48.

Warlick, D. (1998). *Raw materials for the mind: Teaching and learning in information and technology rich schools.* Raleigh, NC: The Landmark Project.

Wiggins, G., & McTighe, J. (1998). *Understanding by design.* Alexandria, VA: Association for Supervision and Curriculum Development.

Wolfe, P. (2001). *Brain matters* (p. 142). Alexandria, VA: Association for Supervision and Curriculum Development.

Resources

Bangert-Downs, R. L., Kulik, C. C., Kulick, J. A., & Morgan, M. (1991). The instructional effects of feedback in test-like events. *Review of Educational Research, 61*(2), 213-238.

Benzwie, T. (1996). *More moving experiences.* Tucson, AZ: Zephyr Press.

Campbell, D. (1997). *The Mozart Effect.* New York: Avon Books.

Campbell, B., Campbell, L., & Dickinson, D. (1992). *Teaching and learning through multiple intelligences.* Tucson, AZ: Zephyr Press.

Cummings, A. B. (1998). *Painless fractions.* Hauppauge, NY: Barrons.

Curwin, R. L., & Mendler, A. N. (1997). *As tough as necessary.* Alexandria, VA: Association for Supervision and Curriculum Development.

Farmer, L. S. J. (1999). *Go figure! Mathematics through sports.* Englewood, CO: Teacher Ideas Press/Libraries Unlimited.

Forney, M. (1996). *Dynamite writing ideas: Inspiring students to become authors.* Gainesville, FL: Maupin House.

Goldberg, E. (2001). *The executive brain: Frontal lobes and the civilized mind.* New York: Oxford University Press.

Guild, P. B., & Garger, S. (1991). *Marching to different drummers.* Alexandria, VA: Jarboe Printing Company/Association for Supervision and Curriculum Development.

Haggerty, B. A. (1995). *Nurturing intelligences: A guide to multiple intelligences theory and teaching.* Menlo Park, CA: Addison-Wesley.

Harris, D. E., & Carr, J. F. (1996). *How to use standards in the classroom.* Alexandria, VA: Association for Supervision and Curriculum Development.

Hattie, J. A. (1992). Measuring the effects of schooling. *Australian Journal of Education, 36*(1), 5-13.

Jargodzki, C. P., & Potter, F. (2001). *Mad about physics: Brain-twisters, paradoxes, and curiosities.* New York: Wiley.

Jensen, E. (1998). *Teaching with the brain in mind.* Alexandria, VA: Association for Supervision and Curriculum Development.

Lazenby, G. (1994). The squares of numbers in multiplication: An Ask ERIC Lesson Plan. Retrieved May 29, 2002, from www.askeric.org/virtual/lessons/Mathematics/Arithmetic/ATH0020.html

Leu, D. J., & Leu, D. D. (1999). *Teaching with the Internet: Lessons from the classroom.* Norwood, MA: Christopher-Gordon.

Levine, S., & Johnstone, L. (2000). *Bathtub science.* New York: Sterling.

Majoy, P. (1996). *Riding the crocodile, flying the peach pit.* Tucson, AZ: Zephyr Press.

Marzano, R. J. (2000). *Transforming classroom grading.* Alexandria, VA: Association for Supervision and Curriculum Development.

Murphy, P., Klages, E., Tesler, P., & Shore, L. (1999). *The brain explorer: Puzzles, riddles, illusions, and other mental adventures.* New York: Holt.

Random House Webster's School and Office Dictionary. (2002). New York: Random House.

Rose, L. (1992). Folktales: Teaching reading through visualization and drawing. Tucson, AZ: Zephyr Press.

Sagor, R. (2000). *Guiding school improvement with action research.* Alexandria, VA: Association for Supervision and Curriculum Development.

Saphier, J., & Haley, M. A. (1993). *Activators: Activity structures to engage students' thinking before instruction.* Acton, MA: Research for Better Teaching.

Silberman, M. (1996). *Active learning: 101 strategies to teach any subject.* Boston: Allyn & Bacon.

Spolin, V. (1986). *Theatre games for the classroom: A teacher's handbook.* Evanston, IL: Northwestern University Press.

Sternberg, R. J., & Williams, W. M. (1996). *How to develop student creativity.* Alexandria, VA: Association for Supervision and Curriculum Development.

Stigler, J. W., & Hiebert, J. (1999). *The teaching gap: Best ideas from the world's teachers for improving education in the classroom.* New York: The Free Press.

Sylwester, R. (1995). *A celebration of neurons: An educator's guide to the human brain.* Alexandria, VA: Association for Supervision and Curriculum Development.

Torp, L., & Sage, S. (1998). *Problems as possibilities: Problem-based learning for K-12 education.* Alexandria, VA: Association for Supervision and Curriculum Development.

vos Savant, M. (2000, April 30). "Ask Marilyn" column. *Parade Magazine.*

Warren, J. (1992). *1-2-3 math: Pre-math activities for working with young children.* Torrance, CA: Totline.

Wujec, T. (1988). *Pumping ions: Games and exercises to flex your mind.* New York: Doubleday.

Index